TO

FROM

DATE

Enjoy life sip by sip not gulp by gulp.

THE MINISTER OF LEAVES

drinking

tea

Take a Little Time for Tea

ARTWORK BY

Kathy Hatch

HARVEST HOUSE PUBLISHERS

EUGENE, OREGON

Take a Little Time for Tea

Copyright © 2009 by Harvest House Publishers
Eugene, Oregon 97402
www.harvesthousepublishers.com

ISBN 978-0-7369-2372-9

Artwork© by Kathy Hatch and used by Harvest House Publishers, Inc., under authorization from
MHS Licensing, Minneapolis, Minnesota. For more information regarding art prints featured in this
book, please contact:

> MHS Licensing
> 11100 Wayzata Blvd., Suite 550
> Minneapolis, MN 55305
> (952) 544-1377
> www.mhslicensing.com

Design and production by Koechel Peterson & Associates, Inc., Minneapolis, Minnesota

Harvest House Publishers has made every effort to trace the ownership of all poems and quotes. In the
event of a question arising from the use of a poem or quote, we regret any error made and will be pleased
to make the necessary correction in future editions of this book.

Printed in China

09 10 11 12 13 14 15 / LP / 10 9 8 7 6 5 4 3 2 1

Teapot is on, the cups are waiting,
Favorite chairs *anticipating*.
No matter what I have to do,
My *friend*, there's always time for you.

AUTHOR UNKNOWN

What better way to
suggest friendliness—
and to create it—than with
a cup of tea?

J. GRAYSON LUTTRELL
1930

There is no place I'd rather be,
than here with friends
having tea!

LEMON TEA

4

Serve sticks of *peppermint*
or lemon *candy* with cups of hot tea.

Guests stir, sweeten, and *flavor* their tea

all at once—and no spoons to wash.

AUTHOR UNKNOWN

LEMON TEA

INGREDIENTS:

2 cups boiling water

2 peppermint tea bags

2 tablespoons lemon juice

fresh mint sprigs

* Serves Two *

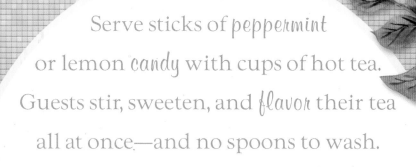

Springtime
lemon cake

INGREDIENTS:

1 package yellow cake mix
1 11-ounce jar lemon curd (divided)
1 cup whipping cream
1 tablespoon powdered sugar

DIRECTIONS:

Lightly grease and flour a 9 x 13 baking dish.
Prepare cake mix per package instructions.
Add 8 ounces of lemon curd, mix well.
Bake cake according to package instructions.
Cool cake and refrigerate. Beat whipping cream
until soft peaks form. Fold in remaining
lemon curd and powdered sugar.
Frost top of cake and keep refrigerated.
This cake is best if prepared one day in advance.

Very little is needed to make
a happy life. It is all within yourself,
in your way of thinking.

MARCUS AURELIUS

"Take some more tea," the March Hare said to Alice.
"I've had nothing yet," Alice replied
in an offended tone, "so I can't take more."
"You mean you can't take less," said the Hatter.
"It's very easy to take more than nothing."

LEWIS CARROLL
Alice's Adventures in Wonderland

To have tea in perfection, it is only necessary to observe the following rules:

1 * Draw fresh, cold water from the faucet.

2 * Bring the water to a bubbling boil.

3 * Use one teaspoonful of tea for each cup of water required, and if too strong, reduce the quantity.

4 * Use a porcelain or china pot, which has been warmed beforehand.

5 * Pour the furiously boiling water over the tea leaves and let it steep for not less than four and not more than six minutes.

6 * Pour off the liquid into another heated porcelain or china vessel, and don't use the discarded leaves again.

English Rose Tea

INGREDIENTS:

1/2 cup dried Red Rose petals
2 tablespoons dried Lemon Balm
1 tablespoon dried Rosemary

DIRECTIONS:

Mix together. Use 1 teaspoon per 1 cup boiling
water. Steep for 5-8 minutes.
Sweeten with honey.

*Where there's tea
there's hope.*

SIR ARTHUR PINERO

HONEY

There are few hours
in life more *agreeable* than the
hour dedicated to the *ceremony*
known
as *afternoon tea.*

HENRY JAMES

11

What **kind** of teapot
makes the best tea? Most experts
would say that *silver*, silver plate,
and stainless steel are very good, if kept
properly cleaned out; that there is nothing
wrong with aluminum, provided that it is *aluminum*
of good *quality*; and that *enamel* is hard wearing
but liable to chip and, if chipped, it makes poor tea.
But the experts' final word would probably
be that *china* or earthenware is the best
material of all, and that there is, in fact,
nothing to equal…our old friend
the brown *earthenware* teapot.

GERVAS HUXLEY
Talking of Tea

Tea beckons us to enjoy quality time
with friends and loved ones, and especially to
rediscover the art of relaxed conversation.

DOROTHEA JOHNSON
Tea & Etiquette

14

CHOCOLATE
Covered Strawberries

DIRECTIONS:

Dip washed strawberries in melted chocolate.
Set on waxed paper to dry. Place chocolate
covered strawberries on a pretty
plate, dust edge of plate with
cocoa powder, and add a
dollop of fresh whipped
cream in center of plate.

Serve with Strawberry Iced Tea

*It isn't the big pleasures
that count the most; it's making
a great deal out of the little ones.*

JEAN WEBSTER

15

Perhaps that is the true gift of a teatime celebration:

It fills our cups with joy and warmth and friendship.

May the echo of the teacups' message be heard

not only at Christmas, not only on special occasions,

but anytime friends come together.

EMILIE BARNES

Strawberries

Tea, heav'ns delight, and nature's truest wealth...the drink of love.

PETER ANTOINE MOTTEUX

Strawberry
iced tea

INGREDIENTS:
1 pint fresh strawberries
$1/2$ cup sugar
5 cups boiling water
5 tea bags—Black Tea
1 can frozen lemonade concentrate
1 quart sparkling water

SWEET Strawberry TEA

DIRECTIONS:
Clean strawberries, remove stems, and cut into quarters. Place strawberries in bowl, cover with sugar, and let set to coat. Steep tea bags in boiling water 5-7 minutes. Remove tea bags and let water cool. Add strawberries to cooled tea, mix in thawed lemonade concentrate. Chill. When ready to serve, add sparkling water and pour over ice into individual glasses.

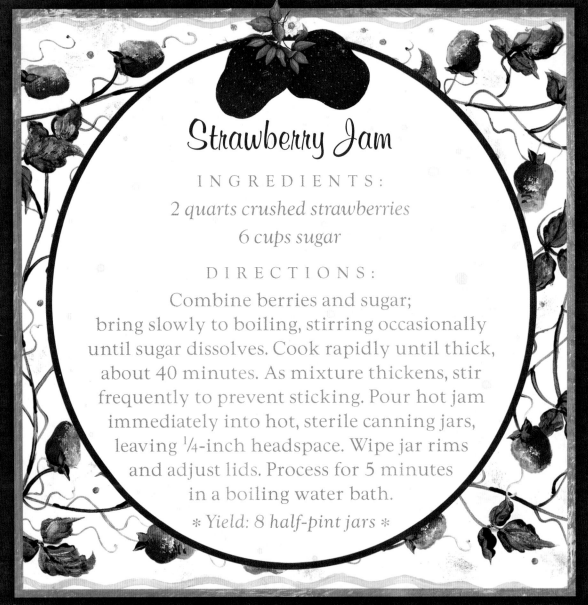

Strawberry Jam

INGREDIENTS:

2 quarts crushed strawberries
6 cups sugar

DIRECTIONS:

Combine berries and sugar;
bring slowly to boiling, stirring occasionally
until sugar dissolves. Cook rapidly until thick,
about 40 minutes. As mixture thickens, stir
frequently to prevent sticking. Pour hot jam
immediately into hot, sterile canning jars,
leaving $\frac{1}{4}$-inch headspace. Wipe jar rims
and adjust lids. Process for 5 minutes
in a boiling water bath.

* Yield: 8 half-pint jars *

I love the little **joys** of life—
The **smell** of rain, the **sound** of brooks,
The taste of crispy toast and **jam**,
The **sight** of rows and rows of books.

REBECCA MCCANN

If prepared from leaf not too strong, such tea, when poured into a shallow cup, will be found to be of a beautiful amber color and daintily aromatic. Poured into a deep cup, the same brew will appear darker in hue. A hint to the tea lover: Serve always in shallow cups, as then the aroma spreads and assails the nostrils more temptingly.

H. IRVING HANCOCK
"The Harmless Drinking of Tea" * *Good Housekeeping*, 1909

Tea is mankind's oldest established and most loved beverage because a cup of tea is good to the taste and because it makes life more pleasant by the feeling of well-being that it gives to mind and body.

GERVAS HUXLEY
Talking of Tea

You can never get a cup of tea large enough or a book long enough to suit me.

C. S. LEWIS

Say, is there *beauty* yet to find?
And certainty? And quiet kind?
Deep *meadows* yet, for to forget
The lies, and truths, and pain?…*oh!* yet
Stands the church clock at ten to three?
And is there *honey* still for tea?

RUPERT BROOKE

It is the simple things of life that make living worthwhile, the sweet fundamental things such as love and duty, work and rest and living close to nature.

LAURA INGALLS WILDER

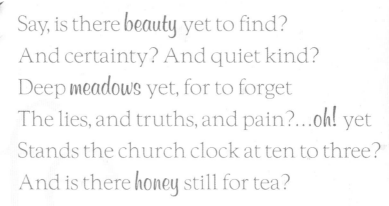

Strange how a teapot
can represent at the same time

the comforts of solitude and

the pleasures of company.

AUTHOR UNKNOWN

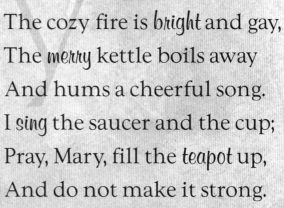

The cozy fire is *bright* and gay,
The *merry* kettle boils away
And hums a cheerful song.
I *sing* the saucer and the cup;
Pray, Mary, fill the *teapot* up,
And do not make it strong.

BARRY PAIN

Blackberry Tea

HEALTH BENEFITS:

*Blackberries are rich
in antioxidants
and vitamins A and C.*

Blackberry Tea

Herbal
Tea
CAFFEINE
FREE

12oz

Loose Leaf

Sweet, fruity taste
Enjoy hot or over ice

DIRECTIONS:

Pick blackberry leaves and dry them
in the sun. When dry, crumble with
mortar and pestle. Use 2 teaspoons
of leaves per cup of boiling water.
Steep for 8-10 minutes. Strain.

HERBAL TEAS

*Made from edible flowers, herbs, leaves, roots,
bark, or berries. Naturally caffeine free,
soothing, and relaxing.*

WHOLE GRAIN
Blackberry Muffins

INGREDIENTS:

1 cup whole wheat flour

1 cup quick oats

1 tablespoon baking powder

$1/2$ cup honey

$1/3$ cup raisins

$1 1/2$ cups blackberries

1 cup water

$1/3$ cup oil

3 eggs

$1/2$ cup chopped walnuts

Bread and water can so easily be toast and tea.

AUTHOR UNKNOWN

26

DIRECTIONS:

Mix flour, oats, and baking powder together.
In a separate bowl, mix honey, water, oil, and eggs.
Add liquid mix to dry mix and blend well.

Stir in blackberries,
raisins, and walnuts.
Spray muffin tins
with nonstick spray.
Spoon muffin mix
into tins and bake
at 400 degrees for
30 minutes.

The ability to simplify means
to eliminate the unnecessary so that
the necessary may speak.

HANS HOFMANN

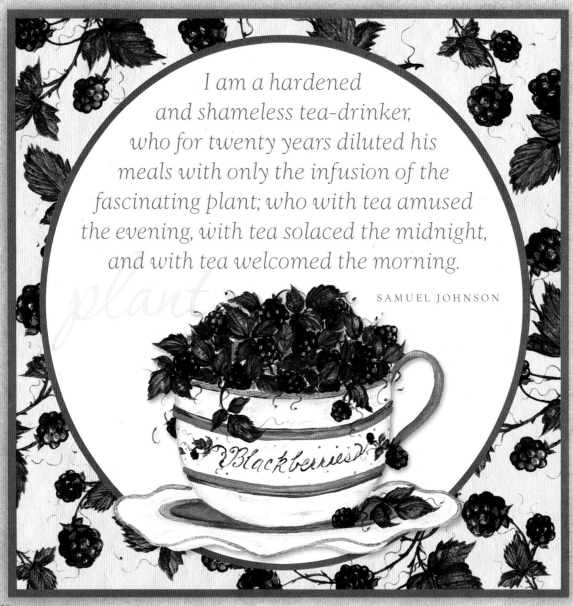

I am a hardened
and shameless tea-drinker,
who for twenty years diluted his
meals with only the infusion of the
fascinating plant; who with tea amused
the evening, with tea solaced the midnight,
and with tea welcomed the morning.

SAMUEL JOHNSON

Blackberries

Read this, my dears, and you will see
how to make a nice cup of tea.
Take teapot to *kettle*, not t'other way round
and when you hear that *whistling* sound
pour a little in the pot
just to make it nice and hot.
Pour that out and put in the tea,
loose or in bags, your *choice*, you see.
One bag for each two cups will do
with one extra bag to make a fine *brew*.
Steep 3 to 5 minutes, then pour a cup.
Then sit right down and *drink* it up!

PATRICIA WINCHESTER
"Afternoon Teas"

Somehow taking tea together encourages

an atmosphere of intimacy when you slip off

the timepiece in your mind and cast your fate

to a delight of tasty tea, tiny foods, and thoughtful conversations.

GAIL GRECO

Blueberry
tea cake

INGREDIENTS:

1 egg

$^2/_3$ cup sugar

1 $^1/_2$ cups flour

2 tablespoons baking powder

$^1/_2$ teaspoon cinnamon

$^1/_2$ teaspoon salt

$^1/_3$ cup milk

3 tablespoons melted butter

1 tablespoon vanilla extract

1 cup fresh blueberries

2 tablespoons sugar

DIRECTIONS:

Beat egg, add $^2/_3$ cup sugar and milk. Blend well.
Sift together flour, baking powder, cinnamon,
and salt. Add to liquid mix along with melted butter
and vanilla and mix well. Fold in blueberries
with wooden spoon. Pour into 8" square baking pan
that has been greased and lightly floured.
Bake for 25-30 minutes at 350 degrees.

*Never be in a hurry;
do everything quietly
and in a calm spirit.*

ST. FRANCES DE SALES

There is subtle charm in
the taste of tea which
makes it irresistible and
capable of idealization.

OKAKURA KAKUZO

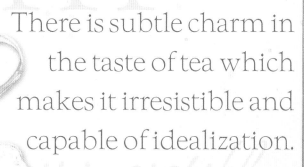

The *variety* of tea is a matter of individual taste.
Of course, I cannot recommend any particular kind,
but I would say that in *your choice* you should not be
influenced at all by other persons' recommendations,
nor at all by fashion, and not much by price.
By this last I mean that you should not think that
a high-priced tea is necessarily any better than one
of lower price which you *fancy*. Select the tea
you like *best* and learn whether it is from an early
or a late picking, its name at home, how it is cured,
and then insist upon getting the same tea every time.
And do not forget that a poor tea *properly made*
is better in every way than a superiour tea badly made.
A few *experiments* with a variety you like will result
in a perfect tea, so far as *your taste* is concerned;
and after that do not modify in any detail
the way of making it properly, for in nothing
is greater *exactitude* required.

OLIVE BROWN SARRE
"The Proper Way to Make Tea" ✷ *Ladies' Home Journal,* 1909

Crystallized
CANDIED
PANSIES

DIRECTIONS:

Dilute an egg white with a few drops of water.
Mix gently together. (Alternatively, you can use
powdered egg whites mixed with water.) Fill a
small bowl with superfine sugar (*not* powdered
sugar). Cover a baking sheet with waxed paper.
Clip flower stems as close to flower as
possible; snip off sepals. Hold what's left of
the stem with tweezers. Using your fingers
or a small paintbrush, coat the entire
flower with the egg white mixture.
Next, hold the flower over
the bowl of sugar

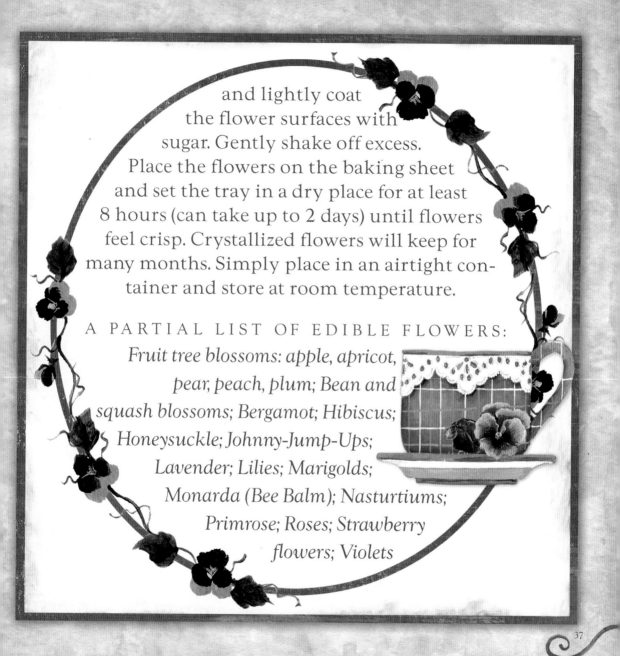

and lightly coat
the flower surfaces with
sugar. Gently shake off excess.
Place the flowers on the baking sheet
and set the tray in a dry place for at least
8 hours (can take up to 2 days) until flowers
feel crisp. Crystallized flowers will keep for
many months. Simply place in an airtight con-
tainer and store at room temperature.

A PARTIAL LIST OF EDIBLE FLOWERS:
*Fruit tree blossoms: apple, apricot,
pear, peach, plum; Bean and
squash blossoms; Bergamot; Hibiscus;
Honeysuckle; Johnny-Jump-Ups;
Lavender; Lilies; Marigolds;
Monarda (Bee Balm); Nasturtiums;
Primrose; Roses; Strawberry
flowers; Violets*

Tea is drunk to forget the din of the world.

T'IEN YIHENG

Surely everyone is aware of the divine pleasures which attend a wintry fireside; candles at four o'clock, warm hearthrugs, tea, a fair tea-maker, shutters closed, curtains flowing in ample draperies to the floor, whilst the wind and rain are raging audibly without.

THOMAS DE QUINCEY

warmth

The tea party is a spa for the soul. You leave your cares and work behind. Busy people forget their business. Your stress melts away, your senses awaken.

ALEXANDRA STODDARD

The daintiness and yet elegance
of a china teacup focuses one to be gentle,
to think warmly, and to feel close.

CAROL & MALCOLM COHEN

She herself alone distributed the cups of tea
from the big red pot before her, which, although
the weather was warm, was covered, when not in use,
with a flannel cozy made in the form of a rooster.

MURIEL CAMPBELL DYAR
"The Tea Party" ✳ *Harper's Monthly Magazine*, 1908

Where your pleasure is, there is your treasure;

where your treasure, there your heart;

where your heart, there your happiness.

AUGUSTINE

Chocolate-Cherry Tea Bread

INGREDIENTS:

$1/4$ cup butter

$2/3$ cup sugar

1 egg

2 cups sifted cake flour

1 teaspoon baking soda

$1/2$ teaspoon salt

$1/3$ cup cocoa

1 teaspoon cinnamon

1 cup buttermilk

$3/4$ cup chopped walnuts or pecans

$3/4$ cup dried cherries

DIRECTIONS:

Preheat oven to 350 degrees.

Cream butter and then add sugar, a bit
at a time, and mix well after each addition.
Add the egg and beat well. Mix and sift
together flour, baking soda, salt, cocoa,
and cinnamon. Add to creamed butter and
sugar mixture alternately with the buttermilk,
beating well after each addition.
Stir in dried cherries and nuts.

Place batter into a greased bread pan.
Bake at 350 degrees for one
hour or until done.

chocolate

Big Red
Cherry
TEA

43

Peter was not very well during the evening.
His mother put him to bed
and made some chamomile tea:
"One table-spoonful
to be taken at bed-time."

BEATRIX POTTER

relax

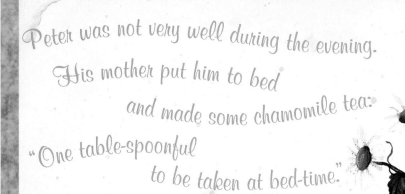

Tea has permeated
the elegance of noble
boudoirs, and entered
the abode of the humble.

OKAKURA KAKUZO

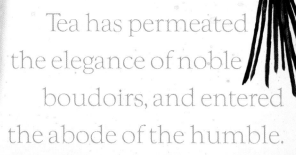

Almond

cake

INGREDIENTS:

1 cup ground almonds

1 cup powdered sugar

8 eggs, separated

1 teaspoon vanilla

$1/2$ teaspoon baking powder

2 tablespoons cocoa

DIRECTIONS:

Blend together ground almonds and powdered sugar.
Add well-beaten egg yolks and vanilla. Sift together
baking powder and cocoa and add to mixture.
Gently fold in stiffly beaten egg whites.
Pour into a well-greased tube pan and bake
at 350 degrees for 30 minutes.

* Serve with whipped cream *

enjoy

If you are cold, tea will *warm* you,
If you are too heated, it will cool you,
If you are depressed, it will *cheer* you,
If you are excited, it will calm you.

GLADSTONE

*What sweet
delight
a quiet life
affords.*

WILLIAM DRUMMOND

cheer

soothing

46

Tea is not just an important article of commerce. Nor is it just an excellent and harmless beverage. If you want to know what tea is, ask the ex-serviceman about his "brew-up" in the desert, or the Londoner about his "cuppa" in the blitz; or find out why the first reaction of millions of ordinary men and women, in joy or in sorrow, whether it be the death of a friend or the telegram announcing a football pool win, is to say, "Let's put the kettle on and have a nice cup of tea."

GERVAS HUXLEY ✳ *Talking of Tea*

47

Chamomile Tea

Chamomile tea is an old-fashioned but efficacious remedy for nervousness. It has a wonderfully soothing effect, making it an excellent bedtime tea.

Calming Chamomile Herbal Tea

INGREDIENTS:

2 tablespoons fresh chamomile flowers

2 cups boiling water

2 thin slices of apple, mashed

1 tablespoon honey

DIRECTIONS:

Steep for 10 minutes. Strain.

*Tea is a work of art
and needs a master hand
to bring out its noblest qualities.*

OKAKURA KAKUZO

remedy

The mere chink of cups and saucers turns the mind to happy repose.

GEORGE GISSIE

sugar

Tea is clearly a most **accommodating** substance. What, amongst so many ways of *drinking tea*, is the "right" way? Strong brew or weak, milk or no milk, **sugar** or no sugar, loose tea or tea bag, **hot** or iced, lemon or mint, or even butter-flavoured? Since so many **different** people are convinced that **their way** is the right way, there can be only one answer to the question. The **right way** to drink tea is the way you like it best.

GERVAS HUXLEY
Talking of Tea

mint

Each cup of tea
represents an
imaginary voyage.

CATHERINE DOUZEL

Green Mint Tea

INGREDIENTS:

10 sprigs of fresh mint
3 teaspoons green tea
3 tablespoons sugar
4 cups boiling water

DIRECTIONS:

Steep for 3-5 minutes,
strain and serve.

The spirit of the tea
beverage is one of peace,
comfort, and refinement.

ARTHUR GRAY

Infuse in hot water
3-5 minutes

Enjoy!

Green Tea

Teatime Cookies

INGREDIENTS:

¾ cup butter

½ cup sugar

2 eggs

1 teaspoon baking powder

3 cups flour

½ teaspoon almond extract

½ cup ground almonds

DIRECTIONS:

Cream butter and sugar together, add well-beaten eggs, almond extract, and ground almonds. Sift flour and baking powder and mix well with butter mixture. Roll out on a floured board and cut with

bake

small round cutter.
Place rounds on greased cookie
sheets, spread a little of the icing on
each and sprinkle with shredded almonds.
Bake at 350 degrees for 10 minutes.

White Icing

INGREDIENTS:

1 egg white
1 3/4 cups powdered sugar
1 teaspoon lemon juice
shredded almonds

DIRECTIONS:

Sift sugar into bowl, add egg white and
lemon juice, and beat for 15 minutes
or until thick. Frost cookies and
sprinkle with almonds.

I smile, of course,

And go on drinking *tea*,

Yet with these April *sunsets*, that somehow *recall*

My buried *life*, and Paris in the Spring,

I *feel* immeasurably at **peace**, and find the world

To be **wonderful** and youthful, after all.

T.S. ELIOT

tea time

There is
no trouble so
great or grave
that cannot
be much
diminished
by a nice
cup of tea.

BERNARD-PAUL HEROUX

56

Ladies of quality became **fascinated** by the drink because, without **clouding** their perception, it **intoxicated** their imagination.

LOUIS WINDMULLER
"The Art of Drinking"
The Forum, 1908

cream

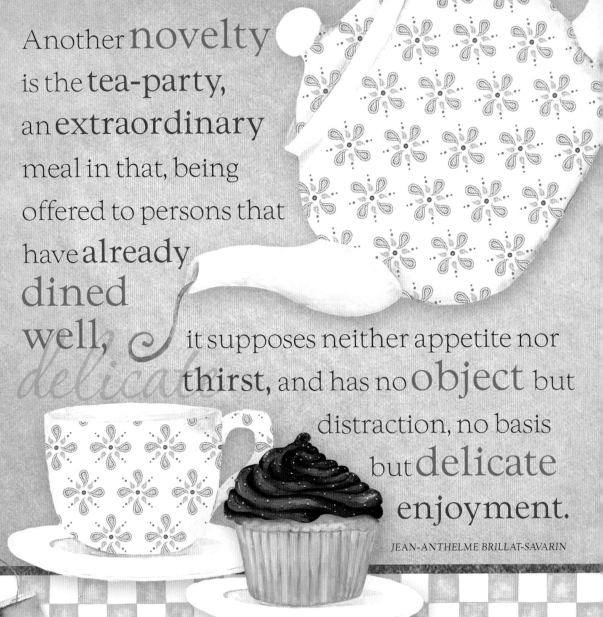

Another **novelty** is the **tea-party**, an **extraordinary** meal in that, being offered to persons that have **already** dined well, _delicate_ it supposes neither appetite nor **thirst**, and has no **object** but distraction, no basis but **delicate** enjoyment.

JEAN-ANTHELME BRILLAT-SAVARIN

Now stir the fire, and close the shutters fast,

Let fall the curtains, wheel the sofa round,

And while the bubbling and loud-hissing urn

Throws up a steady column, and the cups

That cheer but not inebriate, wait on each,

So let us welcome peaceful evening in.

WILLIAM COWPER

Chocolate
CUPCAKE MAKE-AHEAD MIX

INGREDIENTS:

In gallon bag mix together:

$1\,^2/_3$ cups flour

1 cup packed brown sugar

$^1/_4$ cup cocoa

1 teaspoon baking soda

$^1/_2$ teaspoon salt

We'll see if tea and buns can make the world a better place.

KENNETH GRAHAME
The Wind in the Willows

D I R E C T I O N S :

Mark on the outside of each bag, using a permanent marker:

Put ingredients in a mixing bowl and add:

1 cup water

⅓ cup oil

1 teaspoon vinegar

½ teaspoon vanilla

Mix with fork. Lightly spray cupcake tins with oil or use paper baking cups and fill tins two-thirds full. Bake at 350 degrees for 18 to 24 minutes (times vary depending on size of cupcakes). Cool and frost.

WALNUT
Marble Spice Cake

INGREDIENTS:

3 cups flour

3$^{1}/_{2}$ teaspoons baking powder

$^{1}/_{2}$ teaspoon salt

$^{3}/_{4}$ cup butter

1$^{1}/_{2}$ cups sugar

3 eggs

1 cup milk

1$^{1}/_{2}$ teaspoons cinnamon

$^{3}/_{4}$ teaspoon cloves

$^{3}/_{4}$ teaspoon nutmeg

$^{3}/_{4}$ cup finely chopped walnuts

3 tablespoons molasses

DIRECTIONS:

Sift flour, baking powder, and
salt together—set aside.
Cream butter well, add sugar gradually
until light and fluffy. Add eggs one at a time,
beating well until smooth. Add milk alternately
with flour mixture a little at a time until smooth.
Divide batter into two parts. To one portion
of batter add spices, walnuts, and molasses.
Add batter by the $\frac{1}{2}$-cup full into a 9-inch tube pan,
alternating light and dark mixtures.
Bake at 350 degrees for 1 hour.
Cool and frost with your favorite white icing
and decorate with walnut halves.

Come let us have some tea
and talk about happy things.

CHAIM POTOK
The Chosen

tempting

brew

64

vietnamese

vietnamese

a culinary journey of discovery

CORINNE TRANG

Love Food® is an imprint of Parragon Books Ltd

Parragon
Queen Street House
4 Queen Street
Bath BA1 1HE, UK

Copyright © Parragon Books Ltd 2007

Love Food® and the accompanying heart device is a trademark of Parragon Books Ltd

ISBN: 978-1-4054-9564-6
Printed in China

Produced by the Bridgewater Book Company Ltd

Photography: Laurie Evans
Home economist: Carol Tennant

Notes for the Reader
This book uses imperial, metric, and US cup measurements. Follow the same units of measurement throughout; do not mix imperial and metric. All spoon measurements are level: teaspoons are assumed to be 5 ml, and tablespoons are assumed to be 15 ml. Unless otherwise stated, milk is assumed to be whole, eggs and individual vegetables such as potatoes are medium, and pepper is freshly ground black pepper. Recipes using raw or very lightly cooked eggs should be avoided by infants, the elderly, pregnant women, convalescents, and anyone suffering from an illness. The times given are an approximate guide only.

Contents

Introduction

This book will give cooks ranging from enthusiastic beginners to experienced professionals a point of entry to classic Vietnamese cuisine. Inside you will find examples of recipes ranging from the humble home or street-cart cooking through to restaurant specialities. The techniques involved and the ingredients used are fully explained, and tips and variations are also included to offer additional advice and alternatives.

Historical and cultural background

Vietnam sits at Southeast Asia's eastern edge, a cultural crossroads, and its civilization has been forged through millennia of conflict and migration. While its people have historically been beset upon by external forces, they have remained fiercely independent, developing a cuisine unlike any other in Asia. The principal building blocks of Vietnamese cooking are the cuisines of China, South Asia, France, and, to a lesser extent, the United States. An ancient race that mixed with fifty or so other ethnicities, the Vietnamese suffered repeated Chinese conquests for thousands of years, which gave their cooking its Chinese base. In addition, as part of the medieval Khmer Empire, it absorbed the spices and cooking traditions of Cambodia and India. French colonization of Vietnam lasted for a hundred years, starting in the mid-19th century, and added French-influenced dishes and new hybrids. In more recent times, the Vietnam War introduced American fast and snack foods. Globalization has since spread Vietnamese restaurants around the world.

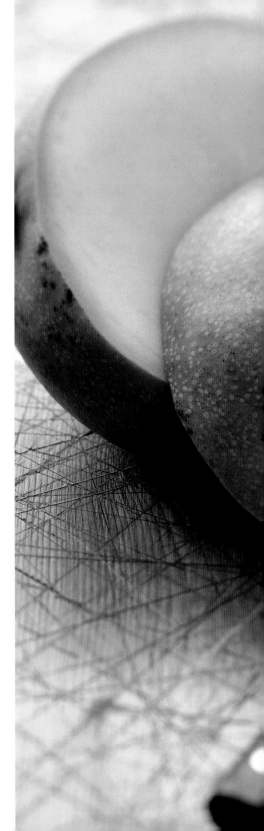

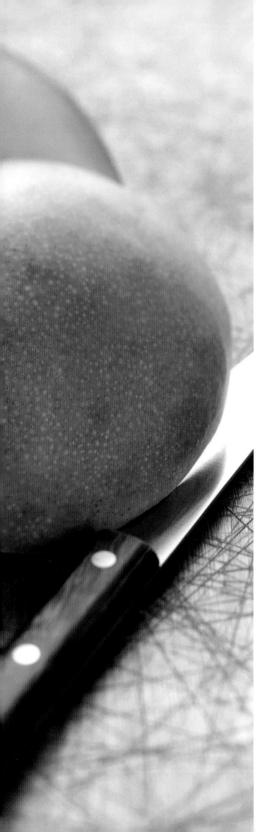

The nature of Vietnamese cuisine

Vietnamese cooking is one of the most highly developed and successful fusion cuisines in the world. National dishes exist, but regional and local variations are an important feature. The Chinese influence is apparent in the use of woks and chopsticks and cooking techniques such as stir-frying and steaming. Chinese-inspired foods such as noodles and spring rolls can also be found in Vietnamese cuisine, as can ingredients such as baguettes, crepes and asparagus, which are French in origin. An Indian influence is reflected in the use of spices, especially in the south where curries are popular.

However, while absorbing these various outside influences, the Vietnamese were able to create a unique cuisine. Unlike many other Asian cuisines, Vietnamese cooking relies on raw vegetables and herbs as counterpoints to cooked foods. For example, many grilled meats and seafood are combined on a plate with raw vegetables and herbs and referred to as *sa lach dia,* or "table salad." In contrast to the spicy curries of Thailand and India, traditionally served with rice, Vietnamese curries are mild and light, best eaten with French baguettes.

Cooking techniques and flavors

Vietnamese cooking can be experienced by employing simple cooking techniques and explored using mostly basic ingredients. A wok or skillet, saucepan, or broiler is all you need in the way of equipment. While some ingredients will be familiar, others will lead you to enjoy new flavors. You can also sample Vietnamese interpretations of classic French recipes, where local ingredients are creatively applied. For example, in Duck in Orange Sauce (*Duck à l'Orange*), fish sauce has been introduced effectively, and in Braised Beef and Carrots, the subtle flavor of coconut water adds a unique dimension.

Last but not least, take the opportunity to experience familiar cooking techniques in a new context. For instance, *Pho*, the national dish of Vietnam, is a rice noodle soup in which raw ingredients are cooked in steaming broth, and fresh herbs are as important as the seasonings and proteins. If you have ever doubted that soup can make a meal, just try cooking a *Pho!* And then give the rest of the Vietnamese menu a whirl.

Essential ingredients and methods

To cook basic Vietnamese dishes at home, always make sure you have fish sauce, garlic, lemongrass, Thai chiles, ginger, and scallions. But also try the lesser-known store-bought and homemade condiments, herbs, and spices listed below.

Cassia bark

Similar to cinnamon sticks, cassia bark is the bark of the evergreen tree, cassia. It is also known as Chinese cinnamon.

Chiles

Thai (or bird's eye) chiles are slender and hot. Red Thai chiles are specified in the recipes, but any color can be used instead. To seed a chile, slice off the stem end and roll the pod between the index finger and thumb, loosening the seeds until they crawl out. Slice the pod into neat rounds.

Fish sauce

Made from fermented anchovies, this is the salt of Vietnam and the backbone of its cuisine. Used at the stove for general seasoning, it is also used as a condiment at the table for last-minute seasoning. Vietnamese, Thai, or Filipino fish sauces are all made from the same ingredients and look the same. Although some may be saltier than others, they are interchangeable. Store for up to six months in a cool, dark

place, or up to nine months in the refrigerator. Fish sauce should be a light to medium caramel color; the older it gets, the darker and more salt-crystallized it becomes. When it turns dark brown to black, it should be discarded.

Fried garlic oil

Fragrant with a rich, roasted, bitter, and sweet flavor, fried garlic oil is mostly used to garnish soups. To prepare, fry 8 finely chopped large garlic cloves in ⅓ cup of vegetable oil in a small saucepan over medium heat for 3 to 5 minutes, or until golden. When serving, include pieces of garlic with each spoonful of oil. Store in the refrigerator for up to one week.

Fried shallots

Shallot rings are added to different foods as a garnish, lending a crunchy texture and sweet flavor. To prepare, thinly slice 8 medium-large shallots and separate the rings. Fry them in ½ cup of vegetable oil in a saucepan over medium-high heat for 3 to 5 minutes, until golden and crisp. Use a slotted spoon to transfer the rings to a plate lined with paper towels to drain.

Green papaya

This fruit, which is eaten as a vegetable, has a dark green skin with a light green flesh. It is used in soups and salads. Its ripe, soft, orange-fleshed cousin is not a substitute. If you cannot find green papaya, use green mango, which is similar in color, or mangoes that are hard to the touch.

Hoisin sauce

This Chinese sweet and salty soybean paste is sold in jars.

Kaffir lime leaves

These leaves have a floral-citrus scent. Dark pine green in color, they grow in the shape of the numeral 8. Count each "double" leaf as a single for any recipe.

Lemongrass

A tall grass with a distinct citrus flavor, lemongrass is very fibrous. Remove the bruised outer leaves and cut off the hard root and dry, tough green tops. Use the remaining lower white to light green stalk, measuring 6 to 8 inches/15 to 20 cm long. Grate for adding to marinades, thinly slice for stews, such as curries, or crush for flavoring stocks.

Rice paper

Soak dried rice paper in room-temperature water for 1 to 2 minutes, until pliable, but separate them and add one at a time to keep them from sticking together. When ready to use, lay flat and blot dry so they are sticky but not slippery.

Rice noodles

Soak dried rice noodles in room-temperature water for about 30 minutes, or until pliable, then cook them in boiling water for 3 to 5 seconds for vermicelli, or 5 to 10 seconds for medium or large sticks, which resemble Italian linguine in shape only.

Saw leaf

This fragrant green leaf, similar in taste to cilantro, is long and narrow with a serrated edge. It can be found in Asian or Latin markets.

Scallion oil

This oil is used as a last-minute flavoring. Cooking the scallions removes their pungent note, letting their sweet character come to the fore. To prepare, trim and slice the scallions into ¼-inch/5-mm thick pieces. Fry in ⅓ cup of vegetable oil in a small saucepan over medium heat for 2 to 3 minutes, or until fragrant and wilted. When serving, be sure to include both fragrant oil and scallion pieces. Store in the refrigerator for up to one week.

Star anise

A spice widely used in Asian cuisines, its aroma is similar to black licorice. Use it whole, and add to soups and stews.

Stocks

Simmer rather than boil stocks to keep them clear. To remove the fat, lay a paper towel on top of the stock to absorb the fat, then lift off and discard. Repeat with clean paper towels until the fat is almost all removed. Alternatively, refrigerate the stock until the fat solidifies, then break up and discard. Store stocks in the refrigerator for up to three days, or freeze for up to three months.

Tamarind concentrate

Sold in jars, tamarind concentrate is sour with a subtle sweet note. It is as thick as creamy soup and dark brown in color, and is free of the fibers and seeds found in the fresh pods or tamarind pulp sold in blocks. If using the pulp, add $\frac{1}{2}$ cup of pulp to 2 cups of hot water and mash to loosen the pulp. Strain through a fine strainer and collect the concentrate (about $2\frac{1}{3}$ cups), then discard the solids.

Thai basil

Used in the cuisines of Southeast Asia, Thai (or Asian) basil has a distinct licorice-like flavor. Italian basil is not a substitute. If you cannot find Thai basil, use cilantro or mint for an authentic Asian flavor substitute.

Toasted rice flour

This is used to add flavor to meatballs and seafood quenelles. Toast 1 cup of long-grain rice in a dry skillet over medium heat for 15 minutes, or until a rich golden color, shaking the pan to avoid burning the grains. Transfer to a spice grinder and process to a fine powder consistency similar to espresso ground coffee. Store in a cool, dark place for up to three months.

Soups, Rice,
and Noodles

Rice forms part of nearly every Vietnamese meal, not only in rice dishes but rice-based noodles, often added to soups, rolls, and crepes, which all feature here in this collection of simple-to-prepare, flavorful dishes.

Recipes include Rice Noodle Soup with Beef, the famous northern soup; *Pho*, where slices of tender steak are cooked in steaming stock; and fragrant, palate-cleansing clear soups, as well as crisp-coated chunks of fish served over noodles. There are also some real showstoppers: lacy Vietnamese crepes make an elegant meal in themselves, while spring and summer rolls deliver restaurant flair at home, and beef fondue is the perfect dish for relaxed entertaining.

Spicy and sour fish and pineapple soup

Canh ca nau dua

Serves 6

1 lb/450 g skinless, boneless catfish or cod fillets, cut into large chunks

1/3 cup tamarind concentrate

8 oz/225 g peeled and cored ripe pineapple, cut into bite-size chunks

1 large ripe tomato, peeled, halved, seeded, and cut into 8 wedges

2 or more red Thai chiles, seeded and thinly sliced into rounds

1 tbsp fish sauce

12 fresh Thai basil leaves, freshly torn

6 fresh saw leaves, freshly torn, or 1/3 cup fresh cilantro leaves

salt and pepper

Fried Garlic Oil, for garnishing

Light fish stock

3 quarts water

2 1/2 lb/1.1 kg fish heads and bones

1 oz/25 g fresh ginger, peeled and thinly sliced

4 scallions, trimmed and crushed

2 to 3 tbsp fish sauce

Sour soups are popular in Southeast Asia for their cooling effect. In Vietnam, this chile-spiced fish and pineapple version has a distinct tamarind flavor. It is sipped like a beverage as a palate cleanser throughout the meal.

For the stock, put the water, fish heads and bones in a large saucepan and bring to a boil over high heat. Reduce the heat to medium-low, then add the ginger, scallions, and fish sauce, and simmer for 1 1/2 hours, or until reduced by about half, skimming off any foam. Strain the stock, discarding the solids, and remove any fat.

Season the fish with salt and pepper to taste. Cover with plastic wrap and refrigerate for up to 30 minutes.

Pour the stock into a medium saucepan and bring to a gentle boil over medium heat. Reduce the heat to medium-low, then add the tamarind concentrate, pineapple, tomato, chiles, and fish sauce and cook for 10 minutes. Add the fish chunks and cook for 5 minutes, or until opaque and fork-tender.

Ladle the soup into small individual bowls. Scatter over the torn basil and saw leaves and drizzle with Fried Garlic Oil to garnish. Serve immediately.

Asparagus and crab soup

Sup cua mang tai

Serves 6

2 to 3 cups cooked fresh crabmeat

2 cups fresh white or green asparagus, cut into 3/4-inch/2-cm pieces

2 large egg whites, lightly beaten

1 tbsp cornstarch

2 tbsp water

salt and pepper

1/2 cup fresh cilantro leaves, for garnishing

Chicken or crab stock

3 quarts water

2 lb/900 g meaty chicken bones or crab shells

1 oz/25 g fresh ginger, peeled and thinly sliced

4 scallions, trimmed and crushed

2 to 3 tbsp fish sauce

Unable to grow asparagus in Vietnam, where it is known as "Western bamboo," the French imported brined versions, hoping to recreate *Velouté d'Asperge* or creamy asparagus soup. The resulting hybrid is this asparagus and crab combination.

For the stock, put the water and chicken bones or crab shells in a large saucepan and bring to a boil over high heat. Reduce the heat to medium-low and add the ginger, scallions, and fish sauce, then simmer for 1 1/2 hours, or until reduced by about half, skimming off any foam. Strain the stock, discarding the solids, and remove any fat.

Pour the stock into a medium saucepan and bring to a gentle boil over medium heat. Reduce the heat to medium-low, then add the crabmeat and asparagus, and season with salt and pepper to taste. Cover and simmer for 5 minutes, or until the flavors have blended.

Steadily pour the egg whites into the soup, stirring a few times, and simmer for an additional 1 to 2 minutes, or until fully cooked. In a ladle, stir the cornstarch and water together. Lower the ladle into the soup, then stir a few times. Cook until lightly thickened.

Ladle the soup into small individual bowls and scatter with the cilantro to garnish, then serve immediately.

Beef fondue with anchovy and pineapple sauce

Bo nhung dam

A specialty of Vietnam's cattle-raising Northern provinces, this dish is traditionally eaten on special occasions and offered at restaurants specializing in Beef Seven Ways (*Bo Bay Moon*). Beef hot pot is typically the first course.

Serves 6

1 quantity Anchovy and Pineapple Sauce (see Cook's Tip, right)

1 head tender lettuce, such as Boston or oak leaf, leaves separated

1 large carrot, peeled and cut into thin sticks

1 small cucumber, peeled, halved lengthwise, seeded, and thinly sliced into half-rounds

12 sprigs fresh Thai basil, freshly torn

12 fresh saw leaves, freshly torn, or 12 sprigs fresh cilantro, trimmed and chopped

4 oz/115 g dried rice vermicelli, soaked in water until pliable and drained

24 dried rice paper triangles

1¹/2 to 2 lb/675 to 900 g eye of round steak, thinly sliced

Vinegar broth

1 tbsp vegetable oil

1 lemongrass stalk

2 large garlic cloves, crushed

1 large shallot or ¹/2 small red onion, thinly sliced

1¹/2 cups rice vinegar

1 cup water

¹/4 cup granulated sugar

¹/2 tsp toasted sesame oil

For the vinegar broth, heat the vegetable oil in a fondue pot set in the center of the dining table. Meanwhile, discard the bruised leaves and root end of the lemongrass stalk, then halve and crush 6 to 8 inches/15 to 20 cm of the lower stalk. Add the garlic, shallot, and lemongrass to the oil and stir-fry for 5 minutes, or until fragrant and golden. Add the vinegar, water, sugar, and sesame oil and boil gently.

Arrange the lettuce, carrot, cucumber, basil, and saw leaves in individual piles on a large platter.

Bring a medium saucepan of water to a boil over high heat. Put the vermicelli in a strainer. Lower the strainer into the water and cook the vermicelli for 3 to 5 seconds, or until al dente. Lift the strainer out and transfer the vermicelli to a serving dish.

Separate and soak 1 or 2 rice papers at a time in a large baking dish half-filled with room-temperature water for 1 to 2 minutes, or until pliable. Drain, then arrange overlapping next to the vegetables on the platter.

To eat, cook 2 to 3 slices of beef in the vinegar broth for 15 to 30 seconds, or until medium-rare. Take a rice paper, line it with a lettuce leaf, and top with the cooked beef, followed by small amounts of the vermicelli, carrot, cucumber, basil, and saw leaves. Wrap the rice paper to enclose the ingredients and dip in the sauce.

Cook's Tip

To make the Anchovy and Pineapple Sauce, put 1 cup peeled, cored, and finely chopped ripe pineapple; 6 anchovy fillets packed in oil, drained and bones removed; 1 large garlic clove, crushed and finely chopped; and 1 teaspoon granulated sugar in a mortar, then pound to a chunky paste with a pestle. Add 1 red Thai chile, seeded and finely chopped; 1 tablespoon rice vinegar; and ¹/4 cup freshly squeezed lemon juice. Pound to distribute evenly. Transfer to a serving bowl.

Rice noodle soup with beef

Pho bo

Serves 6

1 small to medium yellow onion, peeled, halved, and thinly sliced

2 cups mung bean sprouts

12 sprigs fresh Thai basil, torn

12 fresh saw leaves, freshly torn, or 12 sprigs fresh cilantro, trimmed and chopped

4 red Thai chiles, seeded and sliced into thin rounds

2 limes, each cut into 6 wedges

1 package (1 lb/450 g) medium dried rice sticks, soaked in water until pliable and drained

1 lb/450 g eye of round steak, thinly sliced

Fried Shallots, for garnishing

hoisin sauce, for serving

Beef stock

4 lb/1.8 kg oxtail

4 quarts water

1 large onion, peeled

6 whole cloves

4 oz/115 g fresh ginger, peeled, sliced, and crushed

6 star anise

1 piece cassia bark or cinnamon stick, 3 to 4 inches/7.5 to 10 cm long

2 tbsp fish sauce, plus extra to taste

salt and pepper

Referred to as *Soupe Tonkinoise* by the French Colonials, *Pho* was originally considered a breakfast or snack food. Today, this sweet and savory, fragrant soup, which "cooks" its ingredients in the serving bowl, is also eaten for lunch or dinner.

For the stock, blanch the oxtail in a large saucepan of boiling water for 15 minutes and drain. Rinse the saucepan and return the oxtail with the measured fresh water. Bring to a boil over high heat, then reduce the heat to medium-low. Add the whole onion studded with the cloves, and the ginger, star anise, cassia bark, and fish sauce, and season with salt and pepper to taste. Simmer for 3 hours, or until reduced by about half, skimming off any foam. Strain the stock, discarding the solids, and remove any fat.

Pour the stock into a large clean saucepan and bring to a gentle boil over medium heat. Adjust the seasoning with fish sauce to taste and add the sliced onion.

Arrange the bean sprouts, basil, saw leaves, chiles, and lime wedges in individual piles on a large platter.

Bring a medium saucepan of water to a boil over high heat. Put a handful of rice sticks in a strainer. Lower the strainer into the water and cook the noodles for 5 to 7 seconds, or until al dente. Lift the strainer out and transfer the noodles to a large soup bowl. Repeat 5 more times for a total of 6 servings.

Top each of the 6 servings of noodles with 8 overlapping slices of the raw beef. Ladle 1½ cups of the stock (including some onions) over each serving.

To eat, scatter the soups with bean sprouts, basil, saw leaves, chiles, and Fried Shallots, and squeeze over juice from the lime wedges to taste. Serve with hoisin sauce on the side for dipping the beef.

Rice noodle soup with shrimp, squid, and pork

Hu tieu do bien

Serves 6

1 small to medium yellow onion, peeled, halved, and thinly sliced

2 cups mung bean sprouts

12 sprigs fresh Thai basil, freshly torn

12 fresh saw leaves, freshly torn, or 12 sprigs fresh cilantro, trimmed and chopped

4 red Thai chiles, seeded and sliced into thin rounds

2 limes, each cut into 6 wedges

1 package (1 lb/450 g) medium dried rice sticks

18 small to medium raw jumbo shrimp, peeled and deveined

12 large scallops, halved

12 cleaned baby squid, cut into 1/2-inch/1-cm wide rings

Fried Garlic Oil, to taste

Pork stock

1 medium dried squid

3 lb/1.3 kg lean pork ribs, separated

1 cup preserved daikon

2 tbsp fish sauce, plus extra to taste

1 tbsp thick soy sauce (optional)

salt and pepper

This delicious soup of rice noodles with seafood and pork is a specialty of the South. The broth, made with dried squid, pork bones, and preserved daikon, is sweet and savory. Served with herbs, fresh lime juice, and sliced chiles, it offers a spicy finish.

For the pork stock, using tongs, char the dried squid over an open gas burner, turning often to avoid overburning. When cool enough to handle, peel or scrape away the charred very thin skin.

Put the squid, pork ribs, preserved daikon, fish sauce, and soy sauce, if using, in a large saucepan and bring to a boil over high heat. Reduce the heat to medium-low and adjust the seasoning with salt and pepper to taste, then simmer for 3 hours, or until reduced by about half, skimming off any foam. Strain the stock, discarding the solids, and remove any fat.

Pour the stock into a large clean saucepan and bring to a gentle boil over medium heat. Adjust the seasoning with fish sauce to taste and add the sliced onion.

Arrange the bean sprouts, basil, saw leaves, chiles, and lime wedges in individual piles on a large platter.

Bring a medium saucepan of water to a boil over high heat. Put a handful of rice sticks in a strainer. Lower the strainer into the water and cook the noodles for 5 to 7 seconds, or until al dente. Lift the strainer out and transfer the noodles to a large soup bowl. Repeat 5 more times for a total of 6 servings.

In the same water, poach the shrimp and scallops separately for 1 minute, or until opaque, then the squid for 30 seconds. Drain and distribute evenly among the noodle servings. Ladle about 1 1/2 cups of the stock (including some onions) over each serving.

To eat, scatter the soups with the bean sprouts, basil, saw leaves, and chiles, then squeeze over juice from the lime wedges and drizzle with Fried Garlic Oil to taste. Adjust the seasoning with fish sauce to taste.

Rice noodles with fried yellow fish, peanuts, and herbs

Cha ca

Serves 6

1 lb/450 g fresh bun, or 1/2 package (8 oz/225 g) dried rice vermicelli, soaked in water until pliable

1/2 cup rice flour or all-purpose flour

1/2 tsp ground turmeric

2 lb/900 g white fish fillets, such as catfish, tilapia, or flounder, cut into 3/4-inch/2-cm cubes

vegetable oil, for deep-frying, plus 2 tbsp for stir-frying

4 scallions, trimmed and cut into 1-inch/2.5-cm lengths

1/3 cup dry-roasted unsalted peanuts

24 fresh Thai basil leaves

24 sprigs fresh dill, trimmed

24 sprigs fresh cilantro, trimmed

salt and pepper

Sweet, Sour, and Spicy Fish Sauce, for serving

The eponymous Cha Ca Street in Hanoi's French Quarter is packed with restaurants serving this wonderful fried fish specialty. Traditionally served over fresh rice noodles called *bun*, the dish is garnished with stir-fried herbs and crushed peanuts.

If the bun has been refrigerated, reheat in boiling water for 2 seconds. Distribute the bun among 6 individual bowls. If using vermicelli, bring a medium saucepan of water to a boil over high heat. Put a handful of vermicelli in a strainer. Lower the strainer into the water and cook the vermicelli for 3 to 5 seconds, or until al dente. Lift the strainer out and transfer the vermicelli to a large soup bowl. Repeat 5 more times for a total of 6 servings.

Put the flour and turmeric in a sealable plastic bag and season with salt and pepper to taste. Shake to mix well. Add the fish cubes, then seal the bag and shake to coat each fish cube evenly.

Heat the oil for deep-frying in a medium saucepan over medium-high heat to 350 to 375°F/180 to 190°C, or until a cube of bread browns in 30 seconds. Working in small batches, take a handful of fish cubes and shake off the excess flour, then lower into the hot oil. Deep-fry for 2 to 3 minutes, or until golden and crisp. Drain on a plate lined with paper towels.

Distribute the fried fish cubes evenly among each noodle serving.

Heat the remaining 2 tablespoons oil in a preheated wok or skillet over high heat. Add the scallions and peanuts, and stir-fry for 1 minute, or until fragrant and wilted. Add the basil, dill, and cilantro and stir-fry for 1 to 2 minutes, or until just wilted. Distribute the stir-fry evenly among each fish and noodle serving and season with Sweet, Sour, and Spicy Fish Sauce to taste.

Spicy chicken and rice porridge with lemongrass

Chao ga

Serves 6

1 lemongrass stalk

2 to 3 red Thai chiles, seeded and sliced into thin rounds

2 cups long-grain jasmine rice

1½ lb/675 g skinless, boneless chicken, sliced

½ cup saw leaves, cut into thin strips, or trimmed and chopped sprigs fresh cilantro, for garnish

1 lemon or lime, sliced into 6 equal wedges, for serving

salt and pepper

Light chicken stock

4 quarts water

2 lb/900 g meaty chicken bones

2 lemongrass stalks

4 scallions, trimmed and crushed

2 to 3 tbsp fish sauce, plus extra to taste

Rice porridge is regarded as comfort food in Asia, where it is often recommended as a palliative when you are feeling less than fully fit. This version is uniquely Vietnamese with the use of lemongrass and hot chiles.

For the stock, put the water and chicken bones in a large saucepan and bring to a boil over high heat. Meanwhile, discard the bruised leaves and root ends of the lemongrass stalk, then halve and crush 6 to 8 inches/15 to 20 cm of the lower stalks. Reduce the heat to medium-low, then add the lemongrass, scallions, and fish sauce, and simmer for 2½ hours, or until reduced by about half, skimming off any foam. Strain the stock, discarding the solids, and remove any fat.

Pour 8 cups of the stock into a medium-large saucepan and bring to a boil over high heat. Meanwhile, discard the bruised leaves and root ends of the lemongrass stalks and finely grate 6 to 8 inches/15 to 20 cm of the lower stalks. Reduce the heat to medium-low, then add the lemongrass and chiles to the stock and simmer for 30 minutes. Season with fish sauce to taste.

Add the rice to the stock and simmer, partially covered, for 1 hour. Add the chicken, stirring to distribute evenly, and cook for an additional 10 minutes. Adjust the seasoning with salt and pepper to taste.

Serve the porridge in individual bowls, scattered with the saw leaves and with juice squeezed over from the lemon wedges.

Chicken, mint, and shallot rice

Rau thom com ga

In this simple, classic recipe, chicken is used to make a broth, which is then used to cook rice. The cooked chicken is then shredded and mixed back into the cooked rice with freshly chopped mint and shallots.

Serves 6

2 cups long-grain jasmine rice

2 to 3 shallots, finely chopped

1 cup fresh mint leaves, chiffonade (see Cook's Tip, right)

Sweet, Sour, and Spicy Fish Sauce, for serving

Light chicken stock

2 quarts water

1 chicken, weighing 2 to 2¹/₂ lb/ 900 g to 1.1 kg

1 oz/25 g fresh ginger, peeled and thinly sliced

4 scallions, trimmed and crushed

2 to 3 tbsp fish sauce

For the stock, put the water and chicken in a large saucepan and bring to a boil over high heat. Reduce the heat to medium-low and add the ginger, scallions, and fish sauce. Simmer for 1¹/₂ hours, or until reduced by about half, skimming off any foam.

Transfer the cooked chicken to a platter and separate the meat from the bones and skin. Shred the meat and set aside. Strain the stock, discarding the solids, and remove any fat.

Put the rice in a bowl and cover with cold water. Swirl the rice to loosen any starch and drain. Repeat twice more until the water runs just clear. Transfer the rice to a large saucepan and add 2³/₄ cups of the stock. Cover and bring to a boil over high heat. Reduce the heat to medium-low and cook for 20 to 25 minutes, or until the stock is fully absorbed. Let rest for 10 minutes, then fluff up the rice with a fork.

Add the shallots, mint, and chicken to the rice and mix well. Serve in individual bowls, drizzled with Sweet, Sour, and Spicy Fish Sauce to taste.

Cook's Tip

To chiffonade the mint, stack the mint leaves together and roll them up tightly lengthwise, like a cigar. Thinly slice crosswise. Do this just as you are ready to add the mint to the rice, otherwise the mint may turn black.

Crispy crepes with pork, shrimp, and bean sprouts

Banh xeo

Makes about 18

1½ cups plain rice flour

¼ tsp ground turmeric

½ cup canned unsweetened coconut milk

vegetable oil, for cooking

12 oz/350 g pork tenderloin, thinly sliced

12 oz/350 g small raw jumbo shrimp, peeled, deveined, and sliced in half lengthwise

3 cups mung bean sprouts

1 head tender lettuce, such as Boston or oak leaf, leaves separated

2 carrots, peeled and cut into thin sticks

1 small cucumber, peeled, halved lengthwise, seeded, and thinly sliced into half-rounds

12 or more sprigs fresh mint, freshly torn

Sweet, Sour, and Spicy Fish Sauce, for serving

Although French derived, these crepes offer typical Vietnamese flavors and textures. The batter is thin, creating a crispy, lacy crepe when cooked. The name *Banh Xeo* is a play on the "sizzling" sound the batter makes as it hits the pan.

Put the flour and turmeric in a medium bowl. Make a well in the center and add the coconut milk. Whisk the dry and wet ingredients together until smooth. Set the batter aside.

Heat 1 to 2 teaspoons of oil in a preheated wok or skillet over high heat, then add the pork and stir-fry for 3 minutes, or until cooked. Transfer to a separate medium bowl. Repeat the process with the shrimp, stir-frying for 1 to 2 minutes, or until opaque, and then the bean sprouts, stir-frying for 30 seconds, or until just wilted. Toss the bean sprouts with the pork and shrimp in the bowl.

Heat 1 teaspoon of oil in an 8-inch/20-cm crepe pan over medium-high heat. Add ¼ cup of the batter while tilting and swirling the pan, working quickly to cover the surface of the pan evenly. Cook the crepe for 3 to 5 minutes, or until the edge lifts and the crepe is crisp. Spread ½ cup of the stir-fried ingredients on one half of the crepe but away from the edge. Fold the other half of the crepe over the filling and transfer to a plate. Repeat with the remaining batter and stir-fried ingredients.

To eat, break off about one-quarter of the stuffed crepe with your hand and place it in the center of a lettuce leaf. Add a small amount each of carrots, cucumber, and mint leaves, then dip in the Sweet, Sour, and Spicy Fish Sauce.

Cook's Tip
Be sure to use plain rice flour instead of "sticky" or "glutinous" rice flour for this recipe. The latter would make the crepes literally sticky.

Crispy crepes with bean sprouts, scallions, and shiitake mushrooms

Banh xeo cai

Makes about 18

1½ cups plain rice flour

¼ tsp ground turmeric

½ cup canned unsweetened coconut milk

vegetable oil, for cooking

3 scallions, trimmed, cut into 1-inch/2.5-cm lengths, and halved lengthwise

3 cups mung bean sprouts

8 to 10 large fresh shiitake mushrooms, stems discarded, cut into thin strips

1 head lettuce, leaves separated

2 carrots, peeled and cut into thin sticks

1 small cucumber, peeled, halved lengthwise, seeded, and thinly sliced into half-rounds

12 or more sprigs fresh mint

Sweet, Sour, and Spicy Fish Sauce, for serving

In this light dish, mung bean sprouts and shiitake mushrooms are stir-fried with scallions, then scattered across a lacy, crispy crepe. The crepe is then folded over the stir-fry, and eaten with lettuce leaves, carrots, and cucumber.

Put the flour and turmeric in a medium bowl. Make a well in the center and add the coconut milk. Whisk the dry and wet ingredients together until smooth. Set the batter aside.

Heat 1 to 2 teaspoons of oil in a preheated wok or skillet over high heat, then add the scallions and stir-fry for 3 minutes, or until wilted. Transfer to a separate medium bowl. Repeat the process with the bean sprouts, stir-frying for 30 seconds, or until just wilted, and then the shiitake mushrooms, stir-frying for 1 to 2 minutes. Toss the mushrooms with the scallions and bean sprouts in the bowl.

Heat 1 teaspoon of oil in an 8-inch/20-cm crepe pan over medium-high heat. Add ¼ cup of the batter while tilting and swirling the pan, working quickly to cover the surface of the pan evenly. Cook the crepe for 3 to 5 minutes, or until the edge lifts and the crepe is crisp. Spread ½ cup of the stir-fried ingredients on one half of the crepe but away from the edge. Fold the other half of the crepe over the filling and transfer to a plate. Repeat with the remaining batter and stir-fried ingredients.

To eat, break off about one-quarter of the stuffed crepe with your hand and place it in the center of a lettuce leaf. Add a small amount of carrots, cucumber, and mint, then dip in the Sweet, Sour, and Spicy Fish Sauce.

Shrimp and pork summer rolls

Goi cuon

Makes 12

4 oz/115 g dried rice vermicelli, soaked in water until pliable and drained

8 oz/225 g pork tenderloin, in one piece

18 small to medium raw jumbo shrimp

1 head tender lettuce, such as Boston or oak leaf, leaves separated, ribs removed

1 large carrot, peeled and cut into thin sticks

1 small cucumber, peeled, halved lengthwise, seeded, and thinly sliced into half-rounds

12 small, thin scallions, trimmed, or 6 large scallions, trimmed and halved lengthwise

24 large fresh mint leaves

12 round rice papers, 8 inches/ 20 cm in diameter

Spicy Peanut Sauce, for serving

A restaurant favorite, these classic rolls can be made successfully at home with a little practice. They are typically dipped in Spicy Peanut Sauce to enhance the different flavors of the ingredients on the palate.

Bring a medium saucepan of water to a boil over high heat. Put the vermicelli in a strainer. Lower the strainer into the water and cook the vermicelli for 3 to 5 seconds, or until al dente. Lift the strainer out and transfer the vermicelli to a large platter. Separate the noodles into 12 equal portions and cover with plastic wrap until ready to use.

Using the same boiling water, cook the pork tenderloin for 20 minutes, or until cooked, then the shrimp for 1 to 2 minutes, or until opaque. Drain and let cool. Slice the pork thinly against the grain. Peel the shrimp and halve lengthwise, then devein.

Arrange the lettuce leaves, carrot, cucumber, scallions, mint leaves, vermicelli, pork slices, and shrimp halves in individual piles on a large platter.

Separate and soak 1 or 2 rice papers at a time in a large baking dish half-filled with room-temperature water for 1 to 2 minutes, or until pliable.

Set a clean dish towel on the counter. When softened, take a rice paper and lay it flat on top of the towel. Blot the paper dry with a second clean dish towel. Working in layers and 1 inch/2.5 cm from the edge of the rice paper closest to you, overlap 3 shrimp halves and top with a lettuce leaf, a portion of vermicelli, some carrot and cucumber, 2 pork slices, and 2 mint leaves. Fold the bottom edge of the rice paper over the filling once tightly and fold in the sides. Add a scallion, making sure the dark green part sticks out on one side, and roll to the end. Repeat with the remaining rice papers and filling ingredients. As you make each roll, soak another 1 or 2 rice papers.

Serve with Spicy Peanut Sauce on the side for dipping.

Tofu summer rolls

Goi Cuon Dau Phu

Makes 12

4 oz/115 g dried rice vermicelli,
soaked in water until pliable
and drained

2 tbsp vegetable oil

1 lb/450 g firm or extra-firm tofu,
drained and sliced into ½-inch/
1-cm thick slices

1 head tender lettuce, such
as Boston or oak leaf, leaves
separated, ribs removed

1 large carrot, peeled and cut into
thin strips

1 small cucumber, peeled, halved
lengthwise, seeded, and thinly
sliced into half-rounds

12 small, thin scallions, trimmed,
or 6 large scallions, trimmed and
halved lengthwise

24 large fresh mint leaves

12 round rice papers, 8 inches/
20 cm in diameter

Spicy Peanut Sauce, for serving

A vegetarian hybrid based on the classic Shrimp and Pork Summer Rolls, this tofu version is equally delicious with the classic Spicy Peanut Sauce (*Nuoc Cham Dau Phong*).

Bring a medium saucepan of water to a boil over high heat. Put the vermicelli in a strainer. Lower the strainer into the water and cook the vermicelli for 3 to 5 seconds, or until al dente. Lift the strainer out and transfer the vermicelli to a large platter. Separate the noodles into 12 equal portions and cover with plastic wrap until ready to use.

Heat the oil in a nonstick skillet over medium-high heat, then add the tofu and pan-fry for 5 to 7 minutes, or until golden and crisp on both sides. Drain on a plate lined with paper towels. Slice in half lengthwise so the tofu resembles large-cut French fries.

Arrange the lettuce leaves, carrot, cucumber, scallions, mint leaves, vermicelli, and tofu slices in individual piles on a large platter.

Separate and soak 1 or 2 rice papers at a time in a large baking dish half-filled with room-temperature water for 1 to 2 minutes, or until pliable.

Set a clean dish towel on the work surface. When softened, take a rice paper and lay it flat on top of the towel. Blot the paper dry with a second clean dish towel. Working in layers and 1 inch/2.5 cm from the edge of the rice paper closest to you, top a lettuce leaf with a portion of vermicelli, some carrot and cucumber, 2 tofu slices, and 2 mint leaves. Fold the bottom edge of the rice paper over the filling once tightly and fold in the sides. Add a scallion, making sure the dark green part sticks out on one side, and roll to the end. Repeat with the remaining rice papers and filling ingredients. As you make each roll, soak another 1 or 2 rice papers.

Serve with Spicy Peanut Sauce on the side for dipping.

Cook's Tip
There are many different types of tofu to choose from. Be sure to choose regular firm or extra-firm tofu; soft and silken types will fall apart when pan-frying.

Pork spring rolls

Cha gio

Makes 36

6 fresh cloud ears (a Chinese fungus), finely chopped, or dried cloud ears

2 oz/55 g dried cellophane noodles, soaked in water until pliable, drained, and chopped

1 lb/450 g coarsely ground pork

1 small yellow onion, finely chopped

1 small carrot, peeled and shredded

1 large egg

36 rice paper triangles, or 9 large round rice papers, 10 inches/ 25 cm in diameter, each quartered into triangles

vegetable oil, for deep-frying

1 head tender lettuce, such as Boston or oak leaf, leaves separated

1 large carrot, peeled and cut into thin sticks

1 small cucumber, peeled, halved lengthwise, seeded, and thinly sliced into half-rounds

1 bunch of fresh mint, leaves removed from sprigs

salt and pepper

Spicy Peanut Sauce, for serving

Filled with pork or a combination of pork and crab, these spring rolls are of Chinese origin. Although relatively easy to prepare, the recipe can be time-consuming, so they are generally reserved for special occasions such as Tet, the Lunar New Year.

If using dried cloud ears, soak in room-temperature water for about 30 minutes, then drain. Put the noodles, cloud ears, ground pork, onion, carrot, and egg in a large bowl. Season lightly with salt and pepper and mix together thoroughly.

Separate and soak 1 or 2 rice papers at a time in a large baking dish half-filled with room-temperature water for 1 to 2 minutes, or until pliable.

Set a clean dish towel on the work surface. When softened, take a rice paper and lay it flat on top of the towel, with the top point closest to you. Blot the paper dry with a second clean dish towel. Put 2 tablespoons of the pork mixture 1 1/2 inches/4 cm away from the top point, shaping the filling into a sausage. Fold the top point over the filling once tightly, fold in the sides, and roll to the end. Repeat with the remaining rice papers and pork mixture. As you make each roll, soak another 1 or 2 rice papers.

Fill about one-third of a medium saucepan with oil and heat over medium-high heat to 350 to 375°F/180 to 190°C, or until a cube of bread browns in 30 seconds. Deep-fry small batches of the spring rolls at a time for 3 to 5 minutes, or until golden and crisp, using tongs or chopsticks to turn the rolls a few times and make sure they do not stick together. Drain on a plate lined with paper towels.

Meanwhile, arrange the lettuce leaves, carrot, cucumber, and mint in individual piles on a large platter.

To eat, put a spring roll in the center of a lettuce leaf with some carrot and cucumber and a mint leaf. Wrap the lettuce leaf to enclose the ingredients and dip in Spicy Peanut Sauce.

Meats and Seafood

Meats and seafood are an integral part of the Vietnamese diet, and here you can sample a variety in a selection of classic dishes, from crisp, pan-fried fish fillets and quickly cooked pork tenderloin, to curried chicken, duck braised with orange, and beef with aromatic spices.

Any of these delicious dishes can be served with rice, noodles, or French baguette. For a simple lunch, select any meat, poultry, or seafood recipe and combine with Pickled Vegetables or a salad such as Green Papaya Salad or Sweet and Sour Cabbage Salad, and serve with rice. For a more elaborate meal, choose one meat or poultry and one seafood recipe, and add stir-fried vegetables, a salad, a clear soup, and plain cooked rice.

Crispy fish with stir-fried tomatoes and herbs

Ca chien sot ca chua

Serves 6

1 cup all-purpose flour

6 catfish, flounder, or tilapia fillets, about 6 oz/175 g each

4 to 6 tbsp vegetable oil

2 large garlic cloves, thinly sliced

4 ripe tomatoes, quartered

1 tbsp fish sauce

12 sprigs fresh dill, trimmed

12 sprigs fresh cilantro, trimmed

12 fresh Thai basil leaves

salt and pepper

For serving

long-grain jasmine rice

Sweet, Sour, and Spicy Fish Sauce

The Mekong River and its Delta are abundant with fish, and catfish is a common menu item. Pan-fried until golden and crisp, the fish in this dish is topped with stir-fried tomatoes and garlic, and garnished with stir-fried herbs.

Put the flour and salt and pepper to taste in a sealable plastic bag. Add the fish and seal the bag, then shake to coat each fish fillet evenly.

Heat 2 tablespoons oil in a skillet over high heat. Working in batches and replenishing the oil as necessary, pan-fry the fillets for 5 to 7 minutes, or until golden and crisp on both sides. Transfer to a serving platter.

In a separate skillet, heat 1 tablespoon oil over high heat, then add the garlic and stir-fry for 3 to 5 minutes, or until just golden. Add the tomatoes and fish sauce and stir-fry for 10 minutes, or until softened. Adjust the seasoning with salt and pepper to taste. Spoon the tomato mixture on top of the fish.

Wipe the skillet clean and heat 1 tablespoon oil over high heat. Add the dill, cilantro, and basil and stir-fry for 1 to 2 minutes, or until just wilted. Scatter over the tomatoes and fish. Serve with jasmine rice and Sweet, Sour, and Spicy Fish Sauce on the side.

Shrimp quenelles

Chao tom

Serves 6

2 lb/900 g raw jumbo shrimp, peeled, deveined, and finely chopped

1/2 cup Toasted Rice Flour

3 tbsp vegetable oil

1 tsp granulated sugar

1 tsp baking soda

2 scallions, trimmed and finely chopped

1 head tender lettuce, such as Boston or oak leaf, leaves separated

1 carrot, peeled and cut into thin sticks

1 small cucumber, peeled, halved lengthwise, seeded, and thinly sliced into half-rounds

12 fresh mint leaves

salt and pepper

Sweet, Sour, and Spicy Fish Sauce, for serving

Shrimp quenelles are a Vietnamese classic. Fresh shrimp is pounded or minced to a fine paste consistency, and seasoned with Toasted Rice Flour and scallions. Traditionally, the mixture is then wrapped around pieces of sugar cane and grilled.

Put the shrimp, 2 tablespoons of the flour, 2 tablespoons of the oil, the sugar, baking soda, and scallions in a bowl. Season lightly with salt and pepper and mix together thoroughly.

Scatter the remaining flour on a plate. Divide the shrimp mixture into 12 equal portions. Shape each into 1½-inch/4-cm long quenelles (or sausages). Roll each quenelle in the flour to coat.

Arrange the lettuce leaves, carrot, cucumber, and mint leaves in individual piles on a large platter, with the Sweet, Sour, and Spicy Fish Sauce in a small serving dish on the side.

Heat the remaining oil in a nonstick skillet over medium-high heat. Add the quenelles and pan-fry, rolling them around, for 5 minutes, or until golden and crisp all over.

To eat, put a quenelle in the center of a lettuce leaf with some carrot and cucumber and a mint leaf. Wrap the lettuce leaf to enclose the ingredients and dip in the Sweet, Sour, and Spicy Fish Sauce.

Pork meatballs

Nem nuong

Serves 6

2 tsp fish sauce

1 tbsp sugar

1 small shallot, finely chopped

1 garlic clove, finely chopped

1 lb/450 g coarsely ground pork

1 head tender lettuce, such as Boston or oak leaf, leaves separated

1 carrot, peeled and cut into thin sticks

1 small cucumber, peeled, halved lengthwise, seeded, and thinly sliced into half-rounds

12 or more fresh mint leaves

1 tbsp vegetable oil

pepper

Spicy Peanut Sauce, for serving

These simple pork meatballs are seasoned with fish sauce and palm sugar, and served with Spicy Peanut Sauce, with fresh vegetables on the side. They can be served as part of a meal or as an hors d'oeuvre for cocktails.

Put the fish sauce and sugar in a bowl and whisk until the sugar is completely dissolved. Stir in the shallot and garlic, and season with pepper to taste. Add the ground pork and mix together thoroughly. Cover and chill in the refrigerator for 1 hour.

Pinch off about 1 tablespoon of the pork mixture and shape into a small meatball. Repeat with the remaining pork mixture.

Arrange the lettuce leaves, carrot, cucumber, and mint leaves in individual piles on a large platter with the Spicy Peanut Sauce in a small serving dish on the side.

Heat the oil in a nonstick skillet, then add the meatballs and cook, rolling them around, for 5 minutes, or until golden all over.

To eat, put a meatball in the center of a lettuce leaf with some carrot and cucumber and a mint leaf. Wrap the lettuce leaf to enclose the ingredients and dip in the Spicy Peanut Sauce.

Grilled lemongrass pork skewers

Suon nuong xa

Serves 6

2 lemongrass stalks

1/4 cup fish sauce

1/4 cup granulated sugar

2 tbsp vegetable oil

2 large garlic cloves, finely grated

1 1/2 to 2 lb/675 to 900 g pork tenderloin, thinly sliced

Sweet, Sour, and Spicy Fish Sauce, for serving

The pork featured here is lean and therefore cooks quickly. For this reason, it is sliced, marinated, skewered, and grilled. The pork can be served with rice and Pickled Vegetables, or atop rice noodles with fresh vegetables and herbs.

Presoak 24 or more bamboo skewers, about 8 inches/20 cm long, in water for 30 minutes.

Meanwhile, discard the bruised leaves and root ends of the lemongrass stalks, then finely grate 6 to 8 inches/15 to 20 cm of the lower stalks. Put the fish sauce and sugar in a bowl and whisk until the sugar is completely dissolved. Add the oil, lemongrass, and garlic and stir well. Add the pork and mix to coat the pieces fully. Cover and let marinate in a cool place for 20 minutes.

Prepare an outdoor charcoal grill or preheat a gas broiler to medium-high heat, or preheat a nonstick grill pan over medium-high heat. Meanwhile, drain the skewers, then thread the marinated pork onto the skewers.

Grill the skewered pork for 1 to 2 minutes on each side, until cooked and crisp. Serve with Sweet, Sour, and Spicy Fish Sauce for dipping.

Braised pork shanks in caramel sauce with eggs

Thit heo kho nuoc dua

Serves 6

1/3 cup granulated sugar

2 tbsp water

3 cups coconut water (not coconut milk) or plain water

1/2 cup fish sauce

3 lb/1.3 kg pork shanks with rind, bone in

6 scallions, trimmed and crushed

2 oz/55 g fresh ginger, peeled, sliced, and crushed

6 large garlic cloves, crushed

4 dried red Chinese (tien sien) chiles

6 star anise

1/2 tsp five-spice powder

6 eggs, hard-cooked and peeled

This pork dish is derived from a similar Chinese specialty. The primary differences are that the soy sauce is replaced with fish sauce, and coconut water is used instead of water. Spiced with star anise, chiles, and lemongrass, this makes a hearty meal.

Cook the sugar and water in a large saucepan over medium heat for 8 minutes, or until the sugar has melted and turned medium-brown in color. Turn the heat off and stir in the coconut water and fish sauce.

Melt the hardened caramel over medium-low heat. Add the pork shanks, turning to coat each piece all over with the sauce, scallions, ginger, garlic, chiles, star anise, and five-spice powder. Simmer for 4 hours, or until the meat is fork-tender.

Add the eggs, turning them to coat all over with the sauce, and simmer for an additional 5 minutes, or until the egg whites become a deep caramel color. Skim the fat off the top before serving.

Cook's Tip

Leaner cuts of pork, such as pork butt (shoulder), can be used if cut into large chunks. However, the gelatinous pork shank is the more desirable and a classic cut for this braised dish. The eggs should be eaten in small bites with sauce to moisten their otherwise dry texture, which is the result of their having been cooked twice.

Chicken curry

Cari ga

Serves 6

2 lemongrass stalks

¼ cup vegetable oil

3 large garlic cloves, crushed

1 large shallot, thinly sliced

2 tbsp Indian curry powder

3 cups canned unsweetened coconut milk

2 cups coconut water (not coconut milk) or chicken stock

2 tbsp fish sauce

4 fresh red Thai chiles or dried red Chinese (tien sien) chiles

6 kaffir lime leaves

6 boneless chicken thighs or breasts, 6 to 8 oz/175 to 225 g each, with or without skin, cut into 2-inch/5-cm pieces

1 large white yam or sweet potato, peeled and cut into 1-inch/ 2.5-cm chunks

2 Asian eggplants, cut into 1-inch/2.5-cm pieces

2 cups green beans, trimmed

2 carrots, peeled and diagonally cut into ½-inch/1-cm thick pieces

For garnishing

12 fresh Thai basil leaves, lightly crushed

Fried Shallots

This Vietnamese chicken curry is delicate in comparison to the more widely known Thai curries. The sweet and savory broth is coconut milk seasoned with Indian curry powder, fish sauce, and lemongrass. Fried shallots and herbs are used as garnish.

Discard the bruised leaves and root ends of the lemongrass stalks, then slice 6 to 8 inches/ 15 to 20 cm of the lower stalks paper thin.

Heat the oil in a large saucepan over high heat, then add the garlic and shallot, and stir-fry for 5 minutes, or until golden. Add the lemongrass and curry powder and stir-fry for 2 minutes, or until fragrant. Add the coconut milk, coconut water, fish sauce, chiles, and lime leaves and bring to a boil. Reduce the heat to low and add the chicken, yam, eggplants, green beans, and carrots. Simmer, covered, for 1 hour, or until the chicken and vegetables are fork-tender and the flavors have blended.

Serve, garnished with the basil leaves and Fried Shallots.

Roasted garlic poussins

Ga nuong toi

Serves 6

1 cup mushroom soy sauce

¹/₂ cup palm sugar or light brown sugar

2 tbsp vegetable oil

6 large garlic cloves, finely grated

2 tbsp coarsely ground black pepper

6 poussins, 6 to 8 oz/175 to 225 g each, or 12 quail, about 3 to 4 oz/85 to 115 g each

This marinade is used throughout Southeast Asia, most often for small birds such as young chicken, but it is also delicious with strong-flavored meats, such as duck or hanger steak. This dish is generally served with Pickled Vegetables and rice.

Preheat the oven to 450°F/230°C.

Meanwhile, put the soy sauce and sugar in a large bowl and whisk until the sugar is completely dissolved. Add the oil, garlic, and pepper, and stir well. Add the poussins or quail, turning to coat evenly. Loosen the skin of the birds, if using, to allow the marinade to penetrate. Cover and let marinate in the refrigerator for 30 minutes to 1 hour.

Set a roasting rack in a roasting pan. Arrange the poussins breast-side down, and roast in the preheated oven for 30 to 45 minutes, or until tender, the juices run clear when a skewer is inserted into the thickest part of the meat, and the skins are crisp. After 20 minutes, turn the poussins breast-side up.

If roasting quail, roast for 5 to 7 minutes, breast-side down, then 10 to 15 minutes, breast-side up, until tender, the juices run clear when a skewer is inserted into the thickest part of the meat, and the skins are crisp.

Duck in orange sauce

Vit nau cam

Serves 6

1 tbsp vegetable oil

6 duck legs (thighs and drumsticks), 6 to 8 oz/175 to 225 g each

2 lemongrass stalks

8 large garlic cloves, crushed

2 oz/55 g fresh ginger, peeled and thinly sliced

6 scallions, 4 trimmed and crushed, 2 trimmed and thinly sliced diagonally

4 cups freshly squeezed orange juice

freshly squeezed juice of 2 limes

1/4 cup fish sauce

1 tbsp granulated sugar

1 tsp five-spice powder

6 star anise

4 fresh red Thai chiles or dried red Chinese (tien sien) chiles

2 to 3 cups water

salt and pepper

This duck dish, braised with orange juice and spices, is derived from the French classic *Canard à l'Orange*. Cooked until the meat just about falls off the bones, it is delicious served with rice and Stir-Fried Leafy Greens.

Heat the oil in a large saucepan over high heat then add the duck legs and cook for 20 minutes, or until crisp all over, cooking the first side until crisp and coming off the bottom of the pan easily, then turning over and cooking the other side.

Meanwhile, discard the bruised leaves and root ends of the lemongrass stalks, then halve and crush 6 to 8 inches/15 to 20 cm of the lower stalks.

Transfer the duck legs to a plate. Drain off most of the fat from the saucepan, leaving about 1 tablespoon in the pan. Heat over high heat, then add the garlic, ginger, and crushed scallions and stir-fry for 5 minutes, or until fragrant and golden. Add the orange juice, lime juice, fish sauce, sugar, five-spice powder, lemongrass, star anise, and chiles.

Reduce the heat to medium-low and return the duck legs to the saucepan. Add enough water to cover by about 1 inch/2.5 cm. Simmer, partially covered, for 3 to 4 hours, or until the meat is fork-tender and falling off the bones. Adjust the seasoning with salt and pepper to taste.

Remove the fat and serve garnished with the sliced scallions.

Cook's Tip

Beef shin is a perfect cut for braised dishes and particularly good with this spiced orange sauce. Substitute 3 lb/1.3 kg beef shin, cut into large cubes, for the duck legs. Follow the recipe, braising the meat for 4 to 5 hours.

Braised beef and carrots

Bo kho ca rot

Serves 6

1/3 cup fish sauce

1/4 cup granulated sugar

1 tsp five-spice powder

4 lb/1.8 kg beef short ribs or oxtail, or 3 lb/1.3 kg beef shin, cut into 2-inch/5-cm pieces

3 lemongrass stalks

1 tbsp vegetable oil

8 large garlic cloves, crushed

6 small to medium shallots, peeled

3 oz/85 g fresh ginger, peeled and thinly sliced

5 cups coconut water (not coconut milk) or water

2 to 3 cups water

6 star anise

1 piece cassia bark or cinnamon stick, about 4 inches/10 cm long

4 fresh red Thai chiles or dried red Chinese (tien sien) chiles

4 large carrots, peeled and diagonally cut into 1/2-inch/1-cm thick pieces

salt and pepper

plain boiled rice, for serving

Boeuf aux Carrottes was craved by the Colonial French, and their Vietnamese cooks obliged with their very own variation on the original. Seasoned with fish sauce and spiced with cassia bark, lemongrass, and chiles, this dish packs a lot of heat.

Put the fish sauce and sugar in a large bowl and whisk until the sugar is completely dissolved. Add the five-spice powder and mix well. Add the meat and turn to coat evenly. Transfer the marinade and meat to a sealable plastic bag and seal the bag, then let marinate in the refrigerator, flipping the bag over every hour or so, for 6 hours.

Meanwhile, discard the bruised leaves and root ends of the lemongrass, then halve and crush 6 to 8 inches/15 to 20 cm of the lower stalks.

Heat the oil in a large saucepan over high heat, then add the garlic, shallots, and ginger, and stir-fry for 5 minutes, or until golden. Add the coconut water, water, lemongrass, star anise, cassia, and chiles. Reduce the heat to medium-low and add the meat and marinade and enough water to cover by about 1 inch/2.5 cm. Simmer, partially covered, for 2 hours, then add the carrots. Cook for an additional 2 to 3 hours, or until the meat is fork-tender and falls off the bones. Adjust the seasoning with salt and pepper to taste.

Remove the fat and serve on a bed of rice.

Beef in grape leaves

Bo la lot

Makes 36

1 lemongrass stalk

1¼ lb/550 g lean ground beef

1 large shallot, finely chopped

1 large garlic clove, finely chopped

1 tbsp palm sugar or granulated sugar

1 tbsp fish sauce

36 grape leaves in brine, soaked in several changes of water and drained

2 tbsp vegetable oil, plus extra for oiling grill pan, if needed

Sweet, Sour, and Spicy Fish Sauce

Betel leaves *(la lot)* are not widely available outside of Southeast Asia, but grape leaves are an acceptable substitute. Ground beef is seasoned and then wrapped in the leaves. The resulting rolls are threaded on skewers, grilled, then eaten whole.

Presoak 12 bamboo skewers, about 8 inches/20 cm long, in water for 30 minutes. (It is necessary to skewer the rolls if grilling outdoors—see Cook's tip, right.)

Meanwhile, discard the bruised leaves and root end of the lemongrass stalk, then finely grate 6 to 8 inches/15 to 20 cm of the lower stalk.

Put the ground beef, shallot, garlic, lemongrass, sugar, and fish sauce in a bowl and mix thoroughly—it is best to mix by hand.

Lay a grape leaf flat on a clean work surface, with the pointed tip closest to you. Add about 1 tablespoon of the meat mixture 1 inch/ 2.5 cm from the pointed tip and shape it into a 1½-inch/4-cm long sausage. Fold the pointed tip of the leaf over the filling once, then fold in the sides and continue rolling to the end. Repeat with the remaining leaves and meat mixture.

Prepare an outdoor charcoal grill or preheat a gas broiler to medium-high heat, or brush a nonstick grill pan and preheat over medium-high heat. Meanwhile, drain the skewers. Holding 2 skewers parallel, thread 6 rolls onto the skewers, leaving an ⅛-inch/3-mm space in between each roll to allow the heat through when grilling. Repeat with the remaining skewers and rolls. Brush lightly with the oil.

Grill over the outdoor grill for 2 minutes each side, or until the leaves are crisp, or broil in the grill pan (skewered or not), in batches if necessary, for 2 to 3 minutes each side, or until the leaves are crisp.

Cook's Tip

Flat, wide bamboo skewers are now available that will prevent the rolls from twirling around, which they sometimes do with round skewers.

Condiments and Vegetables

Condiments and vegetables form an important part of Vietnamese cuisine—a humble meal often includes rice together with pickled or stir-fried vegetables and the table condiment *Nuoc Cham*. The lime and fish sauce-based *Nuoc Cham* and the peanut-based *Nuoc Cham Dau Phong* are the most popular sauces, and these can be served to accompany any dish.

Vegetables are eaten fresh, but just as often pickled in rice vinegar and sugar, or freshly tossed in a sauce similar to *Nuoc Cham*. Unripe fruit is also enjoyed in salads, as in the vibrant and refreshing Green Papaya Salad given here. A simple recipe for stir-fried leafy greens is also included, together with a spicy vegetable curry and a pan-fried tofu dish.

Sweet, sour, and spicy fish sauce

Nuoc cham

Makes about 2 cups

3/4 cup fish sauce

1/2 cup granulated sugar

3/4 cup freshly squeezed lime or lemon juice

1 large garlic clove, crushed, sliced, or finely chopped

1 to 2 red Thai chiles, seeded and halved, or thinly sliced into rounds

The ubiquitous table condiment of Vietnam, this sauce is present at virtually every meal. It features lime juice, fish sauce, and sugar, spiced with garlic and chiles. The level of spiciness depends on how these two latter ingredients are prepared.

Put the fish sauce and sugar in a nonreactive bowl and whisk until the sugar is completely dissolved in the fish sauce.

Add the lime juice, garlic, and chiles. Let stand for 20 minutes before serving.

Cook's Tip

There are as many versions of *Nuoc Cham* as there are cooks. Some like the sauce salty, some like it sour, and some like it sweet. It can also be mild or spicy. Adjust the sauce according to personal taste. Note that the more the garlic and chiles are broken down, the spicier the sauce will be; for a mild sauce, be sure to crush, not finely chop, the garlic, and halve the chile pod rather than slicing it into thin rounds.

Spicy peanut sauce

Nuoc cham dau phong

Makes 1½ cups

2 tbsp vegetable oil

1 large garlic clove, finely chopped

³/4 cup dry-roasted unsalted peanuts, ground

1 cup chicken stock

1 cup canned unsweetened coconut milk

¹/4 cup tamarind concentrate

2 tbsp fish sauce

¹/4 cup hoisin sauce

3 tbsp palm sugar or granulated sugar

2 red Thai chiles, seeded and finely chopped

Peanut sauce is popular throughout Southeast Asia. In Vietnam, it tends to be delicate, with chicken stock and tamarind concentrate used to dilute the richness of the basic coconut milk and crushed and puréed peanuts.

Heat the oil in a small to medium saucepan over high heat, then add the garlic and stir-fry for 3 minutes, or until golden. Add the peanuts and stir-fry for 8 to 10 minutes, or until two shades darker and the natural oils start to render.

Add the stock, coconut milk, tamarind concentrate, fish sauce, hoisin sauce, sugar, and chiles. Bring to a boil, then reduce the heat and simmer for 30 minutes, or until reduced by about half.

Cook's Tip

For an instant Vietnamese restaurant-style peanut sauce, stir together ¹/2 cup water, ¹/2 cup hoisin sauce, and ¹/2 cup pure peanut butter.

Pickled vegetables

Rau cai chua

Serves 6

2 large carrots, peeled and cut into thin sticks

1 small daikon (about 1 lb/450 g), peeled and thinly sliced into rounds

1 large ribbed cucumber, such as English Hot House, peeled (optional), halved lengthwise, seeded, and thinly sliced into half-rounds

3 tsp coarsely ground salt

1 cup rice vinegar

1/3 cup granulated sugar

Pickled vegetables are ubiquitous in Vietnamese cuisine. A humble lunch can mean a bowl of rice topped with this popular combination of vegetables, for example, or they may be served as appetizers for more elaborate meals.

Put the carrots, daikon, and cucumber in 3 separate bowls and toss each with 1 teaspoon of the salt. Let stand for 1 hour, tossing occasionally, then drain.

Put the vinegar and sugar in a large, nonreactive bowl and whisk until the sugar is completely dissolved. Add the carrots, daikon, and cucumber and toss well. Let stand for 1 hour, tossing occasionally, then drain before serving.

Cook's Tip
This salad is a great accompaniment to grilled meats or seafood. Store in the refrigerator for up to 2 weeks. For more elaborate, often more festive meals, pickled vegetables can be offered to nibble on as a delicate appetizer.

Sweet and sour cabbage salad

Goi cai

Serves 6

1/2 cup fish sauce

1/2 cup freshly squeezed lime juice

1/2 cup palm sugar or granulated sugar

2 tbsp vegetable oil

3 red Thai chiles, seeded and thinly sliced into rounds

1 small green cabbage, finely shredded (6 cups prepared)

2 large carrots, cut into thin sticks

1 small red onion, finely sliced

12 large fresh Thai basil leaves, freshly torn, or 1/2 cup fresh cilantro leaves

In this salad, shredded cabbage and carrots are tossed in fish sauce, lime juice, and sugar, and spiced with chiles. It can be served on its own, or for a heartier meal, with leftover cooked and shredded chicken, poached shrimp, or sliced pork.

Put the fish sauce, lime juice, and sugar in a nonreactive bowl and whisk until the sugar is completely dissolved. Add the oil, chiles, cabbage, carrots, and onion. Toss well and let stand for 30 minutes to 1 hour.

Drain and serve scattered with the basil.

Variations
To liven up the dining table with vibrant color, substitute red cabbage for the green cabbage. You can also combine half a red cabbage with half a green cabbage.

Green papaya salad

Goi du du

Serves 6

1/2 cup freshly squeezed lime juice

1/3 cup fish sauce

1/3 cup palm sugar or granulated sugar

1 large green papaya, peeled, seeded, and cut into very fine sticks (4 to 6 cups prepared)

2 small carrots, peeled and cut into thin sticks

3 red Thai chiles, seeded and thinly sliced into rounds

1/2 cup dry-roasted, unsalted peanuts, chopped

1/2 cup fresh cilantro leaves, or 12 fresh Thai basil leaves, freshly torn

Green papaya salad is served throughout Vietnam. Tossed with a sweet and sour fish sauce-based dressing, it is wonderfully refreshing. The basic salad is finished with crushed peanuts and Thai basil (or cilantro), and offers earthy, spicy flavor notes.

Put the lime juice, fish sauce, and sugar in a nonreactive bowl and whisk until the sugar is completely dissolved. Add the papaya, carrots, and chiles. Toss well and let stand for 30 minutes.

Drain and serve scattered with the peanuts and cilantro leaves.

Variation
Green mango is a popular substitute for the papaya and is equally delicious when prepared in the same style.

Stir-fried leafy greens

Cai xao

Spinach, bok choy, or Chinese broccoli are stir-fried with oil and flavored with garlic and fish sauce in this simple vegetable dish. However, water spinach is the most typical Vietnamese leafy green vegetable.

Serves 6

2 tbsp vegetable oil

2 large garlic cloves, thinly sliced

1½ to 2 lb/675 to 900 g leafy green vegetables, such as spinach or baby bok choy, leaves separated

fish sauce, to taste

pepper

Heat the oil in a wok or large skillet over high heat, then add the garlic and stir-fry for 3 minutes, or until golden.

Add the leafy green vegetables and stir-fry for 2 to 4 minutes, or until wilted (spinach) and tender (bok choy). Season with fish sauce and pepper to taste.

Cook's Tip
Try the recipe with Asian leafy greens, such as water spinach, which has long, narrow, pointed leaves and hollow stems, or chrysanthemum leaves, which are long and narrow-lobed. Sliced Chinese broccoli can also be stir-fried in the same fashion. If you like a crunchy texture, try snow peas or string beans. If you feel inspired, add 1 cup shiitake mushroom caps cut into thin strips to the mix.

Vegetable curry

Cari cai

Serves 6

2 lemongrass stalks

¼ cup vegetable oil

3 large garlic cloves, crushed

1 large shallot, thinly sliced

2 tbsp Indian curry powder

3 cups canned unsweetened coconut milk

2 cups coconut water (not coconut milk) or vegetable stock

2 tbsp fish sauce

4 fresh red Thai chiles or dried red Chinese (tien sien) chiles

6 kaffir lime leaves

1 carrot, peeled and diagonally cut into ½-inch/1-cm thick pieces

1 small to medium Asian eggplant, cut into 1-inch/2.5-cm pieces

1 small to medium bamboo shoot, cut into thin wedges

1 cup snow peas, trimmed

12 large shiitake mushrooms, stems discarded, caps halved

1 lb/450 g firm or extra-firm tofu, drained and cut into 1-inch/2.5-cm cubes

For garnishing

12 fresh Thai basil leaves, lightly crushed, or ½ cup fresh cilantro leaves

Fried Shallots

Curries are popular in South Vietnam, where Indian-influenced spicy foods are enjoyed. This vegetable and tofu curry can be served with French baguette (the classic way), rice, or noodles.

Discard the bruised leaves and root ends of the lemongrass stalks, then slice 6 to 8 inches/15 to 20 cm of the lower stalks paper thin.

Heat the oil in a large saucepan over high heat, add the garlic and shallot, and stir-fry for 5 minutes, or until golden. Add the lemongrass and curry powder and stir-fry for 2 minutes, or until fragrant. Add the coconut milk, coconut water, fish sauce, chiles, and lime leaves and bring to a boil. Reduce the heat to low, then add the carrot and eggplant, cover, and cook for 10 minutes.

Add the bamboo shoot, snow peas, mushrooms and tofu and cook for an additional 5 minutes.

Serve, garnished with the basil leaves and Fried Shallots.

Cook's Tip

Boiled and vacuum-packed whole bamboo shoots from Japan are the best. These can be sliced and used without any further preparation. If using fresh bamboo, be sure to peel and boil the shoot for 10 minutes in water before using in the recipe. If using frozen raw bamboo, do the same. If using canned bamboo, be sure to use a whole shoot instead of precut shoots. Bamboo shoots have the ability to absorb flavor. For this reason, canned bamboo must be boiled for 2 minutes to eliminate any flavor from the can.

Fried tofu with lemongrass

Dau hu xao xa

Serves 6

3 tbsp fish sauce

3 tbsp freshly squeezed lime
or lemon juice

3 tbsp granulated sugar

1 lemongrass stalk

vegetable oil, for frying

1 large shallot, finely chopped

1 large garlic clove, finely chopped

1 red Thai chile, seeded and
finely chopped

2 lb/900 g firm tofu, drained and
cut crosswise into 1/2-inch/1-cm
thick rectangular slices

6 sprigs fresh cilantro, trimmed,
for garnishing

Tofu was brought to Vietnam from China. It is eaten in soups, braised, or pan-fried, such as in this delicious version topped with a stir-fry of lemongrass, shallots, garlic, and chile.

Put the fish sauce, lime juice, and sugar in a nonreactive bowl and whisk until the sugar is completely dissolved. Set aside.

Discard the bruised leaves and root end of the lemongrass stalk, then finely grate 6 to 8 inches/15 to 20 cm of the lower stalk.

Heat 2 tablespoons oil in a small saucepan over high heat, then add the lemongrass, shallot, garlic, and chile and stir-fry for 5 minutes, or until fragrant and golden. Transfer to the fish sauce mixture and stir well. Set aside.

Working in batches if necessary, heat 2 tablespoons of oil in a nonstick skillet, then add the tofu slices and pan-fry over high heat, turning often, for 6 minutes, or until golden and crisp on both sides. Drain on a plate lined with paper towels. If cooking in batches, add extra oil to the skillet as needed.

Transfer the pan-fried tofu to a serving platter and spoon the herb sauce over each slice, then garnish with the cilantro sprigs.

Sweets

Sweet or dessert items are not traditionally served at the end of a meal in Vietnam. Asian cuisines are characterized by a five-flavor system of sour, sweet, salty, spicy, and bitter notes, and in Vietnamese cooking, sugar is present throughout most meals, so serving a cake as a finale is considered unnecessary. Instead, fresh fruit is eaten to aid digestion.

The dishes in this chapter are served as snacks, often in the afternoon with tea or coffee. Banana is a favored ingredient, paired here with coconut in a sweet tapioca soup, as well as coated whole with batter, deep-fried, and then flambéed. Coconut features again in a colorful drink and is combined with shredded cassava root for a sticky cake.

Banana and coconut tapioca

Che chuoi

Serves 6

3 cups canned unsweetened coconut milk

3 cups water

$1/3$ cup palm sugar or granulated sugar

$1/2$ tsp salt

90 g/$3^1/4$ oz small tapioca pearls

2 ripe bananas, peeled, quartered lengthwise, and cut into $1/2$-inch/ 1-cm dice

toasted sesame seeds, for decorating

A popular dessert throughout Southeast Asia, this banana and coconut tapioca soup is simple to make. The soup may be thick or thin, depending on the amount of tapioca used. It can also be served hot, at room temperature, or lightly chilled.

Pour the coconut milk and water into a medium-large saucepan and bring to a boil over high heat. Reduce the heat to low and add the sugar and salt. While stirring, sprinkle the tapioca pearls into the saucepan in a steady stream. Cook, stirring to keep the pearls from clumping together, for 30 minutes, or until cooked through and fully transparent.

Turn off the heat and add the bananas, then cover. Let the bananas steam for about 10 minutes.

Serve hot, at room temperature, or lightly chilled in individual bowls, lightly decorated with toasted sesame seeds.

Mung bean soup

Che dau xanh

Serves 6

1¼ cups peeled dried yellow split mung beans, soaked in water for 3 hours, then drained

4 cups canned unsweetened coconut milk

⅓ cup palm sugar or granulated sugar

½ tsp salt

toasted sesame seeds, for decorating

Here, dried yellow split mung beans are cooked and puréed, then whisked into palm sugar-sweetened coconut milk. The resulting delicate yellow soup is generally served hot, and is usually enjoyed as breakfast or as an afternoon snack.

Put the mung beans with water to cover by ½ inch/1 cm in a medium saucepan and bring to a boil over high heat. Reduce the heat to medium and cook, stirring occasionally, for 20 to 25 minutes, or until the water is completely absorbed by the beans.

Transfer the beans to a fine mesh strainer set over a bowl. With the back of a spoon, press the beans against the side of the strainer. The result should be a very smooth paste.

Pour the coconut milk into a medium saucepan and bring to a gentle boil over medium heat. Add the mung bean paste, palm sugar, and salt, and whisk to a smooth consistency. Cook for 5 minutes, or until heated through.

Serve in individual bowls, lightly decorated with toasted sesame seeds.

Fried banana dumplings

Chuoi chien

Serves 6

vegetable oil, for deep-frying

1 cup all-purpose flour

2 tbsp granulated sugar

1/2 tsp salt

2 tsp baking powder

2 large eggs

1 1/2 cups canned unsweetened coconut milk

12 small, ripe Asian bananas, peeled

6 tbsp 100%-proof rice alcohol or rum (optional)

For decorating

confectioners' sugar

toasted sesame seeds

A direct take on the French *Bananes Flambées*, fried bananas can be served hot out of the frying oil and drained, or flambéed with rice alcohol or rum. Confectioners' sugar and toasted sesame seeds complete the dish.

Half-fill a small to medium saucepan with oil and heat over medium-high heat to 350 to 375°F/180 to 190°C, or until a cube of bread browns in 30 seconds.

Meanwhile, put the flour, granulated sugar, salt, and baking powder in a medium-large bowl. Whisk to combine the ingredients. Make a well in the center and add the eggs and coconut milk. Whisk, gradually incorporating the dry ingredients into the wet ingredients, until the batter is smooth. Add the bananas to the batter, making sure they are coated evenly all over.

Working in batches if necessary, lower the bananas into the hot oil and deep-fry for 5 to 7 minutes, or until golden and crisp all over. Drain on a plate lined with paper towels. Arrange 2 bananas on each individual dessert plate.

To flambé, fill a tablespoon with rice alcohol and set afire with a match. Scatter the burning alcohol across a serving of bananas. Repeat for each serving, letting the alcohol burn off while the flames dissipate. Decorate with a light sprinkling of confectioners' sugar and toasted sesame seeds before serving.

Coconut yucca cake

Banh khoai mi

Makes one 12 x 9-inch/
30 x 23-cm cake

butter, for greasing

2 cups canned unsweetened
coconut milk

1¼ cups palm sugar or
granulated sugar

½ tsp salt

2 lb/900 g cassava root, bark
removed, shredded (about
5 cups prepared)

Southeast Asian desserts often contain coconut palm sugar and coconut milk because coconut palm are abundant throughout the region. Here, coconut milk, palm sugar, and shredded cassava are combined and baked into a rich, sticky cake.

Preheat the oven to 375°F/190°C. Generously grease a 12 x 9-inch/30 x 23-cm square baking dish with butter.

Put the coconut milk, sugar, and salt in a bowl and whisk until the sugar is completely dissolved. Add the cassava and stir to mix thoroughly.

Pour the cake batter into the prepared dish, spreading it equally throughout. Bake in the preheated oven for 1¼ hours, or until golden brown. Let cool before slicing into approximately 2-inch/5-cm squares.

Cook's Tip
Use a glass baking dish to make sure the cake is browned all around.

Rainbow coconut drink with mango

Che ba mau

Serves 6

1 cup dried adzuki beans, soaked in water for 4 hours and drained

1 cup peeled dried yellow split mung beans, soaked in water for 3 hours and drained

3 cups canned unsweetened coconut milk

1/3 to 1/2 cup palm sugar or granulated sugar

1 tsp salt

1 large ripe mango, peeled, pitted, and diced

toasted sesame seeds, for decorating

crushed ice, for serving

This filling, colorful drink is made with layers of white coconut milk, red adzuki beans, yellow mung beans, and ripe, diced orange mango. It makes for a great afternoon snack and is generally served with crushed or shaved ice.

Put the adzuki beans with water to cover by 2 inches/5 cm in a medium saucepan and bring to a boil over high heat. Reduce the heat to medium and cook, stirring occasionally, for 2 hours, or until the water is completely absorbed by the beans and the beans are cooked through and tender.

Meanwhile, put the mung beans with water to cover by 1/2 inch/1 cm in a separate medium saucepan and bring to a boil over high heat. Reduce the heat to medium and cook, stirring occasionally, for 20 to 25 minutes, or until the water is completely absorbed by the beans.

Put the coconut milk in a small saucepan and bring to a boil over high heat. Reduce the heat to medium-low and stir in the sugar and salt.

To assemble the drink, in individual parfait glasses, and in this order, layer 2 to 3 tablespoons each coconut milk, adzuki beans, crushed ice, coconut milk, mung beans, crushed ice, coconut milk, and mango. Decorate with a light sprinkling of toasted sesame seeds. Serve with a long-stem spoon and a straw.

Sweet milk coffee

Ca phe

Serves 6

6 tbsp canned sweetened condensed milk, or to taste

6 hot double espressos or strong-brewed Thai coffees

ice cubes, for serving (optional)

Condensed milk and strong, dark-roast, espresso-like coffee are stirred together and served hot or iced. Popular throughout Southeast Asia, each cup is made using a single serving, slow-drip French coffee press placed over a coffee cup.

Put a heaping tablespoon of condensed milk (or more to taste) in each of 6 cups. Pour a hot double shot of espresso into each cup and stir.

For iced coffee, half-fill 6 glasses with ice cubes. Pour one cup of stirred espresso and condensed milk over the ice in each glass.

Variation

Substitute strong-brewed black tea (such as gunpowder tea) for the coffee and follow the recipe to make condensed milk-sweetened tea.

Index